Y0-AGU-108

LEGAL
SPECTATOR
&
MORE

Distributed by TheCapitol.Net
PO Box 25706
Alexandria, VA 22313-5706
703-739-3790
www.LegalSpectatorAndMore.com

Softbound ISBN 13: 978-1-58733-009-4
Hardcover ISBN 13: 978-1-58733-179-4

LEGAL
SPECTATOR
&
MORE

Jacob A. Stein

The Magazine Group
Washington, D.C.

*For Mary,
Julie, and
Joseph*

CONTENTS

CONTENTS

This & That

PREFACE

This is the third volume of *Legal Spectator*. Although it includes a few essays from the second volume, this book is made up in the main of articles that appeared in the *Washington Lawyer,* the *American Scholar,* the *Times Literary Supplement,* the *Wilson Quarterly,* and the ABA Litigation Section's publication.

I had the invaluable assistance of an editor's editor, Sharon Congdon. Jeff Kibler designed the book, and it was composed by Brenda Waugh. All are with The Magazine Group.

This book is not copyrighted. Its contents may be reproduced without the express permission of, but with acknowledgement to, the author. Take what you want and as much as you want.

The "Legal Spectator" column in the *Washington Lawyer,* where most of these articles first appeared, commenced some years ago with an article about the need to regild the goddess in Washington, D.C.'s Judiciary Square. Diana was placed in the square as a memorial to J. J. Darlington, a lawyer of yesteryear, but over time, she had lost her beautiful gold covering. After the article appeared, I received calls from people from J. J. Darlington's hometown who were collecting a fund to clean up the statue and reapply the gold. A few weeks ago, I revisited Diana. She is at her golden best. The article that triggered the cleanup is on page 297.

The Foreword to the second volume remains appropriate. Here it is:

The impulse to memorialize in book form transient essays scattered around in periodicals is an impulse that should be suppressed. It should be but seldom is. And so this book.

Everything that follows has appeared before. It is all second-hand. And maybe, some years from now, a battered copy of this book will find its way into the dusty corner of a fine old second-hand bookstore. There it may keep company with William Hazlitt or Logan Pearsall Smith and if good luck holds out it may stand shoulder-to-shoulder with Max Beerbohm. Time and the requirements for shelf space do strange things. Unknown scribblers stand with the very best. Not because merit places them there but because of the fit. This book you hold in your hand is a slim volume. Just the right size to press in at the end of the shelf to keep the other books tightly and nicely in place.

One of these days a tired lawyer, in retreat from the quickly running statute of limitations, and hiding out in a bookstore as I have done, will discover this book. And it may just happen that one or two of the remarks that follow will remind the tired counselor that the ungrateful client, the unresponsive judge, the damnation of deadlines are all common to those of us who must extract a living from the contention of others.

Jacob A. Stein
2003

LAWYERS

WAS IT ME OR MY CASE
THEY DIDN'T LIKE?

The writer's work is given to you between the covers of a book; the painter's on a piece of flat canvas; the actor's in the lineaments of his own face, the port of his own body, the various inflections of his own voice. In criticizing his work, you criticize also him.

Max Beerbohm

The actor's life is one of nagging self-doubt. Some actors try to protect themselves from criticism by adopting an inviolable rule never to read reviews of their performances. If this is not enough protection there is recourse to alcohol. John Barrymore, in real life and in the 1930's movie *Dinner at Eight*, demonstrates the dangers of the alcohol cure.

Lawyers also have a nagging self-doubt—and in a loose way it is comparable to the actor's. Both the lawyer in court and the actor on stage are within a medium that merges with the person. But let me say here that lawyers are not good actors. They are strictly amateurs, second-raters at best. The comparison of the skill of an E. G. Marshall or a Gregory Peck conducting a trial in the movies and a working lawyer conducting a trial in real life proves unfavorable to the lawyer. Nevertheless, there is that loose connection. A bad play and a bad case bring criticism not only of the play and the client but also of the actor and the advocate. Even a good case presents dangers. There are cases that should have been won but are lost. Your adversary makes all the mistakes you hoped he would make. You deliver a marvelous closing argument. You lose. The first time it happens you put it aside as just one of those things. Let it happen twice and you wonder whether there is something about you, as a person, that judges and juries do not like.

To these uncertainties we add a new one: the instant discrediting of the lawyer by the troops of TV legal commentators who know precisely what should have been done and would have been done if only the commentator had been consulted.

When the talk show lawyer completes his media performance and wipes off his makeup he gives no more thought to the matter. The lawyer with a real case must deal with reality. Even when he wins, the client often takes the victory as a foregone conclusion. The client suggests that the case was unnecessarily prolonged and that there should be a public apology together with costs and attorney's fees.

When the case is lost the lawyer is often told by the client and by public sages that the case should have been won. There is yet another indignity that may be awaiting the lawyer who has lost a case. She may read in the press that she is to be replaced by a renowned specialist in post-trial motions.

Some years ago, Joe McMenamin, an excellent lawyer, ran into a losing streak. He decided there must be something about him, the way he handled himself in court, the way he spoke to the judge and the witnesses, that triggered a bad reaction. Here was a lawyer who was as good as a lawyer could be, consumed by self-doubt. In that state of mind he asked friends of his to sit in court and observe him and identify anything he should change.

What we saw when we watched Joe in action was a skillful lawyer. But we did recommend a change. He must get better cases. Joe tried one more case. It was a good case. He won a big verdict, made a big fee and retired to Florida.

The conversation of lawyers and actors reflects their deep insecurity. An actress repeats how she knocked them dead in that last performance. Not only was she good—she was great. She stopped the show. When she got sick they had to close the show. Nobody could replace her. Lawyers are resourceful in finding ways to bring into each conversation how great they were in court. The narrative begins with the difficulty of the case. It was a case that could not be won. But it is won through a marvelous cross-examination that turns the tables. This boasting reveals a yearning, a thirst for flattery, even if it is self-administered.

These days there is an expanding body of literature declaring how important it is for the advocate to wear the correct suit and tie when he goes to court. Some authorities assert it is a mistake to wear dark blue. It is elitist. Gray or green or brown is a better choice. Such colors signal that the advocate is of the common people. And the necktie. Never wear a formal-appearing tie. A solid brown seems to be the winner's choice.

If trials have come to this, then it may be time to revise the process. The fate of a litigant should not turn on such trivia. And I do not think that it does. Most lawsuits settle without trial. The settlement is based on the facts of the case—not on the color of the suit or the tie to be worn at trial.

Nevertheless, there is a reason why the how-to-dress and how-to-present-oneself books are written and sold. They cater to the lawyer's insecurity and his fear that he may offend in some way. He may even believe that there are secrets that great lawyers have and those secrets include subliminal messages that suits and neckties transmit.

I know of only two ways for a lawyer to deal with insecurity and self-doubt. One is temporary, the other permanent. The temporary way is to be honored by the profession, to be given awards in which the words "competence" and "talent" are overused. Along the same line is the induction into legal societies restricted to the elite of the profession. But this is temporary. The next time in court the old anxieties return. The outcome is uncertain. The permanent remedy is to get appointed a judge, preferably with a lifetime appointment. Once a lawyer becomes a judge he can enjoy administering self-doubt, as needed, to those friends at the bar he left behind.

THE "LATE" MR. LeROS

In court the other morning I observed a judge deal with a lawyer who was 10 minutes late for the commencement of a trial. The judge curtly remarked that the tardy lawyer was in contempt and entered a fine of twenty-five dollars. Such an exchange is always thought-provoking.

I was once associated in a case with Hubert LeRos (I do not give his actual name), a talented lawyer whose talents did not include punctuality. The presiding judge was a patient man and he commenced by warning LeRos. The warning worked for a few days and then LeRos faltered. Finally the judge announced that if LeRos were late again, he would hold him in contempt. LeRos was all right from Monday through Thursday.

On Friday, he was late again. When LeRos walked into court, the judge recounted the events and the warnings. He then announced that LeRos was in contempt and fined him fifty dollars. LeRos went to the bench and apologized and requested a hearing. The judge denied the hearing.

The trial of the case continued and LeRos was successful in obtaining a verdict from the jury. After the jury was discharged, the judge asked if LeRos intended to pay the fine. LeRos again requested a hearing and stated that his tardiness was not committed within the presence of the court and therefore was not punishable in a summary fashion. The judge countered by stating that LeRos's absence was in the presence of the court.[1]

The judge by nature was an analytical man and was taken by the ingenuity of LeRos's argument. He asked LeRos to file a statement of his authorities and he would defer ruling.

LeRos put aside all his work and threw himself into researching the problem. He found the authorities at 97 ALR2d 431. After filing his comment he received notice from the court that the contempt finding and the fine were withdrawn and the matter was to be set down for full hearing on the following Monday.

I attended as a spectator, looking forward to a performance by LeRos. At the time set for hearing the judge took the bench but there was no LeRos. The judge patiently waited for 10 minutes and then announced an adjournment.

I called LeRos's office. His secretary told me that he had called her saying that he had been in a traffic accident on the way to court.

The hearing was reset with the additional issue of contempt for failing to appear at the hearing on the initial contempt. LeRos was on time for this and after testimony was taken the judge again found LeRos in contempt for failure to appear at the

---

[1] The judge apparently had in mind *Lyons v. Superior Court*, (Cal) 273 2d 681.

jury trial. He found no contempt for failure to appear at the contempt hearing since LeRos brought in as a witness the operator
of the vehicle that LeRos struck in the collision that caused
LeRos to be late.

Did LeRos deliberately strike the vehicle? I wondered. I am
sure the judge wondered about that, too. The doctrine of proximate cause imposes a policy limitation to shield one from remote
consequences and apparently the judge, applying the doctrine,
gave LeRos the benefit of the doubt.

FAREWELL TO
HUGH LYNCH

As I was walking down K Street one warm summer day in 1950, I was thinking to myself that as a lawyer I had no law practice to speak of and I knew no one of any consequence at the Bar. It was then that Hugh Lynch appeared, introduced himself, and said he had seen me around the courthouse and he wished to know how things were going. Hugh was already an established lawyer with a good practice. He asked if I was available to work on some cases with him. How kind of him to use the word "available." A few days later Hugh did the most marvelous thing one can do for a lawyer: He referred me a case.

After that first meeting I was always on the lookout for Hugh along K Street, and I presumed to elect myself one of Hugh's many friends at the bar. I learned from others that Hugh had been captain of the Princeton tennis team in the early 1930's and as a local tennis celebrity he had a wide circle of friends in the tennis community and friends everywhere else, high up and low down, and the six degrees of separation in between. Each of Hugh's friends discovered independently that Hugh administered a placebo that worked as a things-will-be-better prescription on people.

Hugh also served as a human and humane bulletin board. Friends kept in touch with other friends through Hugh. He was posted on whether the subject of inquiry was in the hospital, coming out of the hospital, out of a job, leaving home, or returning home.

Another of his gifts was an unerring eye for the fraudulent. As a conversationalist, he commenced with some recent incident of fakery or pomposity. This started him off and, as he developed and expanded the absurdity, he brought in speculative farcical subplots until all the possibilities were explored.

Hugh had faith in voodoo medicine. He believed, for instance, that Buddy Goeltz's phenomenal energy was directly related to Buddy's glass of vinegar before breakfast. Hugh was aware that most diseases are iatrogenic, that they originate in doctors' offices. Therefore, to avoid disease, stay away from doctors' offices. It was all right to chat with a doctor in a gin game at Columbia Country Club but not in a professional setting. The voodoo worked for Hugh.

He died just before New Year's last year. He was 81. He continued to play tennis within a few weeks of his heart attack, and he reached his preordained Appointment in Samara with only the narrowest contacts with orthodox medical science.

Occasionally one of Hugh's friends required Hugh's advice concerning an affair of the heart. Back in the 1970's there was a lawyer who found true love late in life. In addition to the problems of an older man in love with an unpredictable young woman, there was the complication that the lawyer was, so his wife thought, happily married. Hugh had lunch with this tortured soul every day for several months. I joined them once or twice. Hugh, in a helpful way, supplied advice concerning *la donna é mobile.* He spoke of the damnably bad luck of finding just the right woman at the wrong time. He expressed some cautionary advice concerning such involvements. Hugh and I later learned that the cautionary advice was ignored. The lovestruck lawyer had taken the love of his life to Mexico. Where did he get the money for such a trip? It came from a client trust account. Hugh then counseled his patient through this additional problem and, in the first stages, it was a suicide watch. Hugh was not one who despaired of the patient because he either was called in too late or the disease seemed incurable.

Hugh's interests included all the popular arts, especially songs and movies of the twenties, thirties, and forties. Among the old movies, he especially liked *Casablanca.* He told me that he had seen *Casablanca* again for the—was it the fifteenth, twentieth, or thirtieth time? He would then hum a few bars of "As Time Goes By"—*A kiss is still a kiss ...* Hugh had trouble recalling the words of the verse of the song, which surprised me. That verse conveyed Hugh's Wordsworthian philosophy: As we lay waste our powers in getting and spending, the world is too much with us. As translated into the poetry of Tin Pan Alley and subject to a faulty memory, my recall of the verse has words deploring:

> *Speed and new invention*
> *And things like fourth dimension*
> *Yet we get a trifle weary*
> *With Mr. Einstein's theory ...*

The last time I saw Hugh was at the corner of Connecticut and K. We made a date for lunch that was never to be. And now

K Street is no longer the magic place where Hugh approaches with a smile of recognition and gesturing, telling me he must convey an insight that just came to him concerning the eternal mysteries of getting clients, the unpredictability of judges, or the great opportunities marriage provides to display maturity of judgment. At such times his happiness was apparent—a happiness based not on his present material circumstances but on some inward serenity, tied to the simple facts of life, uncontaminated by speed and new inventions and things like third dimension.

Whenever Hugh chose to complain, he directed his complaints at the needless, unexplainable cruelty of the everyday world, which he had decided was only a mist obscuring the real world, the wonderful world whose beauty occasionally peaked out as a gracefully executed running forehand stroke on the tennis court, a brilliant comment on the vanity of human wishes, and the wisdom of eluding unnecessary confrontations with people who excuse their meanness by saying, "You must understand that I am the kind of person who always tells the absolute truth, no matter whom it hurts."

IRVING YOUNGER AND JOE DIMAGGIO

The recent TV program replaying the life and times of Joe DiMaggio brought to mind Irving Younger. Mr. Younger frequently worked into his continuing legal education lectures references to Joltin' Joe as the embodiment of perfection in his chosen work.

For those who may not know of Irving Younger, he was, by common consent, the top banana on any CLE program. He brought the law of evidence to life with clever insights, humorous anecdotes, and inside stories. He extracted from the Federal Rules of Evidence a grand unifying theory that reconciles electromagnetism, gravity, and the speed of light.

His Hearsay lecture was unforgettable, and his lecture on the art of cross-examination was even better. Each lecture was worked and reworked so that anything that slowed it down was trimmed off. The final product had the impact of a fine vaudeville act. As he paced the platform he took off his jacket and rolled up his sleeves.

15

To emphasize a point he jumped into the air and screamed the applicable rule. When he completed his four-hour, nonstop lecture, he was the fighter who had gone fifteen rounds. He needed a robe thrown around him and the assistance of two handlers, one with ice water and the other with flattery.

He had excellent credentials. He attended Harvard undergraduate and the New York University Law School. He was an Assistant United States Attorney in Manhattan and thereafter was in private practice. He left private practice to serve as a trial judge in New York City. He then taught trial technique at Cornell, Columbia, Harvard, and Georgetown. In 1981 he joined Williams & Connolly. He left three years later to resume teaching.

In his lectures he reduced the technique of trying a lawsuit into ten black letter rules. Learn them by heart. If you violate them you do so at your client's peril.

He temporarily defrauded his audience of ambitious would-be trial lawyers into believing that each one of them was destined to be a prince of the forum, winning big cases, by following the Younger rules. It was while delivering his exhortations to excellence that he invoked Joe DiMaggio's memory and Joe's perfection in the New York Yankees' outfield and of course Joe's clutch hitting. Younger then shifted to the legendary triumphs of yesteryear's great trial lawyers. There was Max Steuer's cross-examination in the Triangle Shirtwaist company fire case. Max Steuer was defending the factory owners charged with causing the death of factory employees who were unable to flee the burning building because the owners had locked the exits. Steuer's cross-examination consisted of his asking the prosecution's key witness to repeat the story she gave on direct examination. She did so, word for word. That was the cross-examination. Thus, so Irving Younger proclaimed, Mr. Steuer demonstrated that the witness had memorized a story the prosecutor had told her to say.

Mr. Younger gave instances of what happens when the lawyer asks one question too many and converts a good cross-examination into a disaster. And he warned against getting too excited. There was the lawyer who got so excited in arguing an arson case that he exclaimed: "Ladies and Gentlemen, the chimney took fire; it poured out volumes of smoke. Volumes, did I say? Whole encyclopedias, Members of the Jury."

He told of the lawyer who fainted dead away when appearing before Judge Learned Hand.

He preached elegance and relevance and brevity. No wasted motion, just like Joe DiMaggio. He was proud that a case he tried when he was a Williams & Connolly partner gave him the chance to perform like Joe DiMaggio.

He represented The *Washington Post* when it had been sued for libel by the president of the Mobil Oil Corporation. The plaintiff called a trucking executive to the stand. The trucking executive gave testimony helpful to the plaintiff. Mr. Younger's cross-examination consisted of four elegant questions:

Q: Mr. Hoffman, did you just get into Washington about an hour ago?

A: About an hour and a half, I would think.

Q: Did you come up from Florida?

A: No, I did not.

Q: Where did you come from?

A: Indianapolis.

Q: How did you get from Indianapolis to Washington?

A: On the Mobil corporate jet.

"It was a hand grenade in the courtroom," Mr. Younger recalled, "the kind of moment a trial lawyer savors for the rest of his life."

Despite the elegance and brevity of the cross-examination, the jury returned a substantial plaintiff's verdict. When commenting on the verdict in one of his CLE courses he said with a smile that Joe DiMaggio occasionally struck out even though his swing was perfect. Mr. Younger finally prevailed for his client in the court of appeals.

This led to Mr. Younger's warning that the trying of cases requires a tolerance for disappointment. Trying cases is winning and losing. There was a lawyer in New York called Last Chance Levy. He got his cases after the jury returned a guilty verdict. Mr. Levy was the post-verdict and appellate man. He considered himself a winner each day the client was not behind bars. In one of his cases the day came when all appeals ended and the defendant found himself in court for the last time. As he was being led away he whispered to Levy, "What happens now?" Levy answered, "I shall be going to dinner and you are going to jail." Last Chance Levy developed a tolerance for defeat.

After several years in practice Irving Younger returned to his real love, teaching trial practice. Although his life was cut short at age 55, he lives on by and through the videotapes of his great performances, recorded live before spellbound CLE audiences.

CHARLES F. C. RUFF

How can the laborious study of a dry and technical system, the greedy watch for clients and practice of shopkeepers' arts, the mannerless conflicts over often sordid interests, make out a life? Gentlemen, I admit at once that these questions are not futile, that they may prove unanswerable, that they have often seemed to me unanswerable. And yet I believe there is an answer. They are the same questions that meet you in any form of practical life. If a man has the soul of Sancho Panza, the world to him will be Sancho Panza's world; but if he has the soul of an idealist, he will make—I do not say find—his world ideal. Of course, the law is not the place for the artist or the poet. The law is the calling of thinkers. But to those who believe with me that not the least godlike of man's activities is the large survey of causes, that to know is not less than to feel, I say—and I say no longer with any doubt—that a man may live greatly in the law as well as elsewhere.

Oliver Wendell Holmes

I think we would not be doing justice to the feelings many of us have if we passed to the business of the day without taking notice of the fresh gap which has been made in our ranks by the untimely death of Charles Ruff. He, perhaps of all the lawyers among us, came nearest to what every lawyer aspires to be. He was gifted with high intelligence, a sense of self-discipline, and good judgment, all combined with an ease and fluency of delivery. He was, as the general public learned during the impeachment trial, a strenuous fighter. Nevertheless, he leaves behind him no resentments and no enmity. He is taken away in the full tide of a buoyant life still full of promise.

Among his varied professional assignments was the winding up of the Watergate Special Prosecutor's office. Many demanded that a statute setting up the Office of Special Prosecutor, or something like it, was a necessity. Charles Ruff stood against this view. He felt so strongly about it that his final report admonished against any such statute. His advice was ignored. The Special Prosecutor/Independent Counsel statute was enacted. When put into practice it proved how right and farseeing Mr. Ruff was. But only after causing a lot of damage.

He tested his own abilities in many different ways. For a time he served as corporation counsel for the District of Columbia. He also served in the Department of Justice and as United States Attorney. In each he served with quiet distinction.

He was unknown to the general public until the televised impeachment hearings. He made the case for the president. As he spoke he turned over the pages, one by one, of his written statement. The turning of the pages was quite dramatic because he did not look at them. He spoke from memory.

It has been said that the lawyer's role is first to impose order on complicated issues and then present the case with clarity. That is what the public saw. What the public did not see were the hours of preparation required under rigid time constraints for such a performance. The damnable part of the practice of law is that each case requires its own careful laborious preparation. What is learned in the last case cannot be recycled for the next case. There are those who have the capacity—or is it the sense of professionalism?—that compels them to study each case as it comes along as if it were the one and only case. Mr. Ruff had this talent.

In the impeachment trial Mr. Ruff put his client in the best possible light. There was no avoidance of issues. There was no reliance on emotion or special pleading to partisan interests. It was done with dignity and force. It was the work of a gifted professional at the top of his form.

Mr. Ruff appeared in many politically charged cases in addition to the impeachment trial. Anyone who has represented political figures knows how difficult it is when doing so to remain faithful to one's professional obligations. Politicians expect flattery and lawyers are not excluded from these expectations. A lawyer who confronts the facts, confronts them bluntly, may find that he has been replaced by a lawyer who gives false hopes.

In the Lord's Prayer are the words "Lead us not into temptation." Lead us not into temptation. Those are words that define the dangers for a lawyer in the headlines who wishes to remain there. The temptation is to do what is necessary to preserve one's role. A powerful person may hold out the promise of spectacular rewards both in economical terms and in terms of fame and reputation. Mr. Ruff, by reason of his reputation and stature, was beyond the usual lawyerly temptations.

What does the public lose when a fine lawyer is taken from us? Some may say that the public really loses nothing. It just means that somebody with a bad case has one less lawyer he can turn to in order to thwart justice. In some instances this may be true. It does not apply to Charles Ruff. He lent his talents to many worthwhile causes. And those who yesterday could have looked to him for help must now look somewhere else.

GET ME LECHFORD

Gene Fowler's romantic biography of William J. Fallon entitled *The Great Mouthpiece*, published in 1931, set the pattern for the many biographies and "as told to" autobiographies of successful trial lawyers that were to follow.

Invariably, the young legal wizard attracts clients to himself by winning a series of unimportant cases that cannot be won. This brings him the big case. He wins it through various spectacular stratagems of astonishing novelty. He finds himself a celebrity. He leaves his wife.

At this point in the story the author brings in the idiosyncrasies of the hero; his alcoholism, his satyriasis, his flamboyant dress.

At the peak of the hero's popularity his career is threatened, sometimes by his vices, sometimes by charges that he is tampering with juries. Incidentally, William J. Fallon and Clarence Darrow were charged with jury tampering and a good part of their biographies is taken up with a description of their vindication.

The hero in these stories is blessed with a photographic memory and phenomenal powers of concentration, which permit him to memorize overnight the financial statement of the United States Steel Corporation and quote verbatim from page 673 during the cross-examination of the key prosecution witness. The witness is shattered. The hero's client is acquitted and restored to the bosom of his family. The lawyer, in formal dress, accepts the tearful thanks of all and returns to the delightful dinner party from which he excused himself three days before so that he could prepare and try the case.

The drama of the book is heightened by the use of a dramatic title: *The Great Mouthpiece* (William J. Fallon); *Take the Witness* (Earl Rogers); *Final Verdict* (also Earl Rogers); *Hollywood Lawyer* (Milton Golden); *Ready for the Plaintiff* (Melvin Belli); *Never Plead Guilty* (Jake Ehrlich); *Attorney for the Damned* (Clarence Darrow); *Trial Lawyer* (Max Steuer); and *My Life in Court* (Louis Nizer).

You will notice that the name M. Thomas Lechford is not to be found in this list of invincible advocates. This should not be. In addition to the jury triumphs that he has in common with other great lawyers he has an accomplishment that they do not have and no one else shall have in the future. Lechford was the first lawyer disbarred in the New World.

In order to secure information about M. Thomas Lechford one goes to the *Massachusetts Historical Society Collections*, 4th Series, Volume 6 (Boston), 1863. The name of M. Thomas Lechford appears as one who was retained by William and Elizabeth Cole in the summer of 1639 to prosecute a claim against Mrs. Cole's brother, Francis Doughty of Taunton, Massachusetts.

As usual with Lechford, immediately after his emotional closing argument, the jury returned a verdict for Lechford's clients. But juries were returning too many verdicts for Lechford's clients. An investigation was launched. The Massachusetts Historical Records indicate that on September 3, 1639, Lechford was disbarred by the General Court of Massachusetts. The record states, *in haec verba*:

> M. Thomas Lechford for going to the jury, pleading with them out of court, is debarred from pleading any man's case hereafter, unless his own, and admonished not to presume to meddle beyond what he shall be called to by the Courts.

A further examination of the record reflects that Lechford filed a motion for a pardon. The pardon was granted and Lechford resumed the practice of law.

Once again, he was entirely too successful with juries. Once again, there was an investigation. Once again, he was disbarred for "going to the jury, pleading with them out of court."

You would think that this second disbarment would terminate, once and for all, the career of Lechford. You would be wrong. Lechford had the quality common to all great lawyers, persistence. Lechford again petitioned for a pardon and again his petition was granted. He picked up the thread of his career and, as far as available records indicate, he continued as an outstanding trial lawyer.

We have no note concerning Lechford's appearance.

Did he affect cowboy boots and a jumbo-size pocket handkerchief like Jake Ehrlich?

Did he pull on his suspenders during his courtroom speeches like Clarence Darrow?

Did he use a lorgnette like Earl Rogers?

Did he wear black and white shoes, winter and summer, like Jerry Geisler?

Did he cut his own hair like William J. Fallon?

Did he wear huge diamonds, like Howe of Howe and Hummel?

Did he carry his books and files into court in an old brown paper bag like Max Steuer?

No, we have no hint as to Lechford's appearance or his mannerisms. We can only speculate about these things. But maybe Lechford will come to the attention of an imaginative biographer who will supply us the details that will bring to life the personality of M. Thomas Lechford. The plot is there. All it needs is a little beefing up.

It would be best to do it in paperback with an illustration on the cover of Lechford cross-examining a beautiful Indian maiden in an old colonial courtroom. Emblazoned across the maiden's legs, in red letters, would be the title GET ME LECHFORD!

THE DOMESTIC
RELATIONS MAN

Some years ago I represented a woman I shall call Mrs. Corelli in a contested divorce case. I fix the time as 1955. Mr. Corelli was represented by Jean Boardman.

At the time, Jean Boardman was a leader of the local domestic relations bar. He appeared for either the husband or the wife in many of the cases involving those prominent in Washington society. Although I had never met him, I often saw him walking near 15th and H streets where his office was located. His erect posture, his long strides, and his habit of humming and singing as he strode along drew the attention of the passersby.

It was through the Corelli divorce that I met and got to know Boardman. He paid me the honor of dropping by my office one afternoon to discuss settlement. In the course of the discussion I pressed my client's case strongly, and implied that Boardman was representing an unworthy client and he was taking an unworthy, morally questionable position in the litigation. Boardman told me to calm down. He said that if by chance Mr. Corelli, the party who had the money, had hired me instead of Mrs. Corelli, I would be carrying on in the identical immature manner for Mr. Corelli. He added that if the Corelli case were tried instead of settled, I was in for a few surprises. The good sense of what he said made a lasting impression.

As it turned out, the case was tried and I was very much surprised to find that my client had concealed from me a key document.

Thereafter, when I saw Jean striding up and down 15th Street, I walked along with him. I learned that he had come to Washington from the Midwest, employed as a stenographer and secretary to a congressman. His real love was singing. He had wished to take voice training, but it never worked out. While working for the congressman he went to law school. In a relatively short time he built up an active divorce practice, and by 1955 he was one of a small group who were offered the best divorce cases.

I learned also that in a field of practice where the truth is the first casualty, he had established a reputation as a man of unique reliability. He was not a religious man, as far as I could tell, but he was honest by instinct and habit. Judges knew they could take him at his word.

In time we became friends. I saw him often at the courthouse. Here, too, he was in constant motion. He paced the corridors while waiting for his case to be called. As time permitted, he studied looseleaf notebooks he had compiled containing his research into the field of American popular music from the 1890's to the 1940's. He spent his free time in the music division of the Congressional Library, examining old sheet music and copyright records. He knew the details of the lives of many of the early popular songwriters. He was one of the founding members of the Bar-bershop Singing Society and he sang with several of its groups. He knew the lyrics of hundreds of old songs. He was at his happiest singing in his rich baritone voice songs such as "After the Ball Is Over" and "Sweet Adeline."

Once his case was called, there was even more animation. He fingered documents. He opened law books. He gestured. He paced. Each question from the court was responded to with an engaging bluntness.

An expert typist, he did all his own typing. I saw him sit down at his typewriter and bang out agreements, papers, and pleadings. He was brief and persuasive. In fact, in one case he con-vinced a judge in the domestic relations branch of the court to give his client a jury trial. It is set forth in *Rodenberg v. Rodenberg*, 213 A.2d 510 (D.C. 1965). I am told by a knowledgeable practi-tioner that Jean is the only lawyer to have accomplished the feat.

Because of his reputation, he was often asked by those seek-ing judgeships to write letters of recommendation. He routinely refused. He said that on one occasion a defeated congressman's aide had asked for such a letter. Jean said he kept to his resolution of writing no letters, but as he told the story, he did promise that if the gentleman were appointed to the court, he would do the newly appointed judge a favor. He would personally help him find his way to the courthouse.

The last time I saw Jean Boardman he was striding up 15th Street. We chatted, and he told me this story as we walked along, with me a step or two behind. One of his clients, a wealthy wid-ower, was frequently sued for causes sounding in breach of prom-ise by women who produced at trial incriminatory letters. Jean told the gentleman not to compose sweetheart letters. The gentleman said he would follow the advice, but he didn't keep his word. He continued to write letters to his lady friends, addressing them as "My Dear Helen," or "Dear Ruth," or whoever his love of the moment was, but he always added "and Ladies and Gentlemen of the Jury."

Just as I wrote out that recollection I recalled some other advice that domestic relations specialists of years ago liked to give to their clients: "Do right and fear no man. Don't write and fear no woman." You don't hear talk like that any more. Most states have banned by statute the breach-of-promise suit. It is probably wise legislation, but it withdrew from the practice some very interesting litigation.

ATTICUS FINCH, LLP— FORMERLY PC, FORMERLY LLC

Gregory Peck as Atticus Finch in the movie *To Kill a Mockingbird* inspired many people to go to law school. Atticus Finch, the lawyer who stood against bigotry. Atticus Finch, with quiet dignity, ignoring the dangers as he placed himself between the mob and the wrongfully accused. Atticus Finch, the personification of what every lawyer would like to be, at least once in his or her legal career. For one shining moment to be standing up in court speaking eloquently for a just cause rather than sitting in a back room Bates-stamping documents. If there ever was a real-life chance to be the lawyer Atticus was, that chance was substantially reduced by the turn the profession chose to take in 1960.

In the year 1960 the law practice took a giant step away from Atticus. It went corporate. Until the 1960's every law firm practiced as a general partnership. The good thing about a general partnership is that it requires no special meetings of the partners. There is no need for a written partnership agreement. There are no bylaws. There are no employment agreements between the partners. There are no stock certificates to be issued. There is no stock book. There are no filings of the partnership agreement with any governmental agency.

What would Atticus Finch have said if someone were to tell him that the practice of law had turned itself into a corporate enterprise? He might have used the words of Hugo Grotius:

> Lord Coke gravely informs us that corporations cannot be excommunicated, because they have no souls, and they appear to be as destitute of every feeling as if they had also no bowels. There is in truth but one point through which they are vulnerable, and that is the key-hole of the cash box.

Why in 1960 did the law practice go corporate? First, there was a change in the tax laws that gave retirement benefits to a corporation but not to a general partnership. Second, the state legislatures created the professional corporation. It was now legal for professionals such as doctors and lawyers to incorporate. The professionals, instead of being partners, became stockholders and employees of their corporation. As such they were given the retirement tax benefit and certain corporate shield benefits against personal liability. If a malpractice case is filed against the professional corporation, only the assets of the professional corporation and the individual assets of the negligent lawyer alone are available to the plaintiff. All the others get away free. In exchange for these benefits the law firm must indicate its corporateness by the letters PC.

Many lawyers chose to forego the corporate advantages rather than tack on the clanky PC designation. They also objected to all the other things corporations must do: file articles of incorporation, file yearly reports, hold sterile make-believe corporate meetings, draft fictitious corporate minutes, draft employment agreements and talk corporate.

In time the corporate advantages overwhelmed the sentimental resistance to going PC. One general partnership after another converted. Then the complications. Some courts refused to honor the statutory corporate shield. A law firm, so it was said, is subject to a higher law and that higher law requires the law firm, despite its PCness, to put the individual shareholders' personal wealth on the line exactly as general partners do. Clients are entitled to deal with the PC just as they would if there were no PC. Then there was the problem of the lawyer who does little real work and gets paid a large salary by the corporation who discovers that the Internal Revenue Service treats that large salary as a corporate dividend that is taxable first to the corporation and then taxed again to the lawyer employee.

It was also discovered that a PC that breaks up gets little guidance from the existing law. Must the PC redeem stockholder shares? There are odd cases where a stockholder holds stock simultaneously in two professional corporations. The first is the one that he has walked away from and is litigating with, and the second is the one he fled to with all his clients. Courts trying to untangle these issues sometimes ignore the corporate law and apply general partnership law.

With all of this going on, resourceful lawyers decided that there must be an entity that would combine the best of the PC and the general partnership. A new species appeared called the limited liability company. A member of a limited liability company need not worry about shares of stock and corporate charters and shareholders' meetings. In addition, he gets the same protection against malpractice claims as the PC has.

Shortly after the LLC was put on the books, along came the LLP, the limited liability partnership. This has everything the LLC has and picks up the general partnership law to be used to settle disputes. This adds a measure of certainty to the LLP that the LLC does not have. That is good news. The bad news is that the limited liability feature may, as time goes by, destroy the LLP. Here is how it happens:

> A key partnership asset in most law firms is the monies received from Clients for services rendered. Since law firms are not capital-intensive and thus do not need to retain their profits for reinvestment, profits are generally drawn by the partners on a regular basis. In the face of an ongoing negligence lawsuit, negligent partners will have an incentive to retain as much of the profits in the firm while non-negligent or innocent partners will have an incentive to draw as much as possible from the firm. Unlike in the general partnership context where liability rules encourage partners to "sink or swim together," partners in law firms organized as LLPs have divergent incentives based on their differing liability status. [15 Geo. J. Legal Ethics 1 (2001)]

ALL THAT CAN BE SAID

Machiavelli, in a passage which I cannot find, and the Chinese sages agree that certain formalities are necessary before reading or writing can be properly pursued. Al dressed himself after his work in the country, and lit wax candles. The Chinese "sit down before a bright window, at a clean table, burning a stick of incense to dispel anxiety, in order that the fine verses and excellent concepts should take shape." How amused and contemptuous I should once have been of this! I thought I could read or write properly anywhere; yet "if one does not act in this way inspiration will soon be restrained, distracted, dulled or hindered; and how would one then represent the appearances of things and emotions?"

E. M. Forster, Midnight 5/9/36

Lawyers, too, require certain preliminary formalities before getting down to the work of addressing the court. I was in court with one such lawyer the other day. When our case was called, this lawyer cradled in his arms several industrial-strength three-ring binders, two volumes of the *Federal*

Reporter, loose copies of court opinions, scattered tabbed documents, and yellow pads. He deposited this collection on the lectern with loving care. Then, with studied deliberation, he gave an appropriate place to each item. This act of arranging his materials required all his attention. He moved one of the notebooks to the center of the lectern. He opened the notebook and patted it down. He stepped back and looked at what he had done. He approved.

He then smiled and looked up at the judge. Here was the happy advocate, happy to be doing what lawyers are supposed to be doing, standing up in court addressing a federal judge. His pleasure was in the presentation. Winning or losing was incidental.

He began to speak. He cited cases. He referred to footnotes. He discredited a majority opinion. He exalted the dissent by a judge well known to be omniscient. He questioned first principles. He read from and distributed copies of unpublished opinions. He made fine distinctions in the facts. As new arguments suddenly came to mind he paused in awe of his own cleverness. He embellished each with a Paganini variation. Nothing was implausible. All was possible. If he thought the judge might be a member of the Flat Earth Society, he would cite the relevant authorities to prove the judge correct. He prefaced subordinate arguments with the words, "Now this is very important, very important!" He worked in clever requests to reconsider each of his earlier motions that the judge had denied. I was terrified that the judge would take the bait. If he did, the law of the case disappears and I lose several advantages obtained at great cost to my client. I had seen lawyers like this before, lawyers with a gift for speaking fast, convincingly, and interminably. They do well in trial work. A number of them came to the law after a career in religion. As lawyers they utilized powers of persuasion typical of clergymen. Such skill combined with some knowledge of the law and a client in need of jury sympathy makes for an explosive combination. In time they find the law too restraining and they move on to politics or business ventures. As he approached his major theme he became Figaro, the Barber of Seville, singing "Largo al Factotum." When he finished he fell exhausted into his chair at counsel table.

Now it was my turn to address the court. I thought sobriety of speech was in order as a persuasive contrast. But there are judges who are impressed with energetic logomania. The judge we were before had asked my adversary no questions. He had not said, I have heard enough of this nonsense. So I felt it necessary to say a few words. I did and I sat down. My adversary quickly returned to the lectern. He must have the last word. He hoped the judge was like a feather pillow that bears the mark of the last person who sat on him. He said my remarks gave a false impression of the facts and the law. He had the true facts. I was hoping the judge was a scholar and he would give low marks to anyone who uses the phrase "true facts." Doesn't the dictionary define a fact as a true statement? Did the judge pick up those fine points?

Why had I made the mistake of saying anything? Why did I not submit on the papers? The ranting continued. I diverted myself by recalling a description of President Warren G. Harding: *His speeches leave the impression of an army of pompous phrases moving over the landscape in search of an idea. Sometimes these meandering words would actually capture a struggling thought and bear it in triumphantly, a prisoner in their midst until it died of servitude and overwork.*

Reverie was interrupted by my adversary's offer to submit a supplemental memorandum covering points that had arisen at the hearing. The judge gave permission. Then the judge asked me how much time I wished to submit a reply. It was then I decided to show some courage. I said I intended to file no reply. As far as I was concerned, the matter was submitted.

This awakened the judge. He said, "Yes, I think all that can be said has been said. The matter is submitted." That was the first indication that the judge was on the right course. But as of this writing there is no ruling on the motion that was the subject of the oral argument, and there is no ruling on my adversary's supplemental motion for leave to file the attached supplemental memorandum coupled with a supplemental request for an oral hearing.

CIVILITY AS AN ART
FORM IN DIPLOMACY
AND THE LAW

On December 8, 1941, Winston Churchill dispatched a letter to the Japanese Ambassador announcing that a state of war exists between England and Japan. Churchill's letter noted that the Japanese had just bombed Singapore and Hong Kong. Therefore, His Majesty's Ambassador at Tokyo was instructed to inform Japan that a state of war exists between Great Britain and Japan. Churchill ended the letter with these words:

> I have the honour to be, with high consideration,
>
> Sir,
>
> Your obedient servant,
>
> Winston S. Churchill

Churchill commented in his wartime memoirs that "Some people did not like this ceremonial style. But after all when you have to kill a man it costs nothing to be polite." So, we see that even under the most demanding circumstances a resourceful person can discover opportunities to show civility.

Civility in our lives today is sadly lacking, many would agree. In my own profession, the law, the centuries-old tradition of civil discourse between lawyer and judge appears threatened. But before we discuss further civility and the law, permit me to reach back in time to talk about Lord Chesterfield and Benjamin Franklin. Both were lifelong students of the art of civility. Both had illegitimate sons whom they endeavored to train in the art of civility. And both were disappointed by how things turned out with their sons.

Lord Chesterfield, in real name Philip Dormer Stanhope, was born in London in 1694, 12 years before Benjamin Franklin was born in Boston. Chesterfield was a wealthy member of the English aristocracy. During his career he served in Parliament, as a secretary of state, and as the Lord Lieutenant of Ireland. Early in his career, he was ambassador to The Hague when that was an important diplomatic post. While there, he had a love affair with a woman not of his rank or standing. His son, Philip Stanhope, was born of that affair.

Although Lord Chesterfield was noted in his time for his polished writing style, his diplomatic skills, and his sense of honor, he is remembered now chiefly for the letters to his son, Philip. These were triggered by Lord Chesterfield's keen interest in civility, manners, and the social graces, and their role in getting what one wants in this world. He wished his son, who had the disadvantage of illegitimacy, to have the advantage of Lord Chesterfield's experience in the ways of the world. Lord Chesterfield provided tutors to give Philip a thorough grounding in languages, history, travel, and what is now called "political science." While Philip was engaged in educational travel through Europe, and

serving at various minor European diplomatic posts, Lord
Chesterfield transmitted to Philip a father's advice on civility, manners, and the social graces in hundreds of letters. These letters,
written between 1737 and 1768, represent what can be called "the
worldly philosophy," as summarized by Samuel Shellabarger, one
of Chesterfield's biographers:

> It is a belief in the supreme desirability of what most
> men strive for—power, position, wealth, the esteem of
> one's associates, the pleasures of the senses—the pursuit
> and enjoyment of all this to be regulated partly by some
> code of good form and partly by common sense ... The
> objectives of worldliness will always commend them-
> selves to that legal fiction, the ordinary prudent man; its
> value will always seem valuable to 99 per cent of the
> population; it is the most plausible form of selfishness.
>
> The true man of the world is no doctrinaire and
> would warmly disclaim the title of worldly. It may often
> serve his purpose to be considered or consider himself
> an idealist. But his distinguishing features are the same:
> he is the adept of compromise, expediency, the
> unburned bridge, the secret reservation, the ultimate
> confidence in Mammon. It matters not whether or not
> he admits these tendencies to himself, they remain char-
> acteristic of him. It is unnecessary to point out how large
> a section of the great and fair in all generations belong
> to his persuasion. It is one of the most distinguished
> human categories.

The lives of Chesterfield and Franklin raise questions of
whether there is any significant connection between civility and

morality, and whether a high sense of morality could be an imped-iment in serving up all the half-truths and flattery that go with civility. I find that people whose civility is in the first class are gen-erally relativists when it comes to morality. And it often happens that those whose mission is to do good at all times are impatient and rude to their moral inferiors. Such people do not comprehend the nature of civility as an art form.

Lord Chesterfield included in his letters anecdotes and illus-trations to make his point—that one must be attentive at all times to manners—and to emphasize, of course, that one must do noth-ing to be thought a bore. From Bonamy Dobree's *The Letters of Philip Dormer Stanhope*, here is one story Chesterfield related con-cerning that advice:

> Many people come into company full of what they intend to say in it themselves, without the least regard to others; and thus charged up to the muzzle are resolved to let it off at any rate. I knew a man who had a story about a gun, which he thought a good one, and that he told it very well. He tried all means in the world to turn the conversation upon guns; but, if he failed in his attempt, he started in his chair and said he heard a gun fired; but when the company assured him they heard no such thing, he answered, perhaps then I was mistaken; but, however, since we are talking of guns—and then told his story, to the great indignation of the company.

Unknown to Lord Chesterfield, while at one of the minor ambassadorial posts Philip had married a woman well below his own rank and, worse yet, a penniless woman. How unworldly of him. It violated all of Lord Chesterfield's preachments. Lord

Chesterfield did not learn of this until after the death of his son. Philip's young widow arrived at Lord Chesterfield's mansion in London, introduced herself, and presented her babe in arms, Lord Chesterfield's grandson.

Benjamin Franklin came at the subject of civility from a different direction, but, with slight modifications, his view of the world was much the same as Lord Chesterfield's. Franklin, born in 1706, was the fifteenth son of a Boston candlemaker. He worked for a while with an older brother as a printer's apprentice. Franklin could not get along with his brother, his father, or anyone else. As a very young man he decided to leave home and start over. He took a slow boat to Philadelphia and arrived with only a few cents in his pocket. He decided that if he wanted to get ahead he must rid himself of this contrary element in his nature by studying how to get along with people. He became a lifelong student of civility, manners, manipulation, and flattery, just as Lord Chesterfield had. Young Franklin set up a schedule. He would devote time to flattering his way into the circles he wished to enter in order to improve himself by the things he would learn from good company. Franklin also had an illegitimate son, William. When Franklin married, the illegitimate son was raised as if he were born of the marriage.

Franklin, in time, became Philadelphia's leading citizen. In 1757, the colonies sent Franklin to London, where he remained until 1775, trying to work things out between the British and the colonies. While in London, he pulled strings to have his son named as the King's representative for New Jersey. When war was declared, Franklin's son went over to the British. This was a source of great embarrassment to Franklin. He and his son were never to repair the breach.

The difference between Franklin and Lord Chesterfield may be that Franklin was optimistic concerning man's capacity for self-improvement. Chesterfield, like most people of his time, believed that the bad generally overcame the good and that people chose what was best for them when a choice was to be made. That is the way it was and ever would be. Franklin, to the contrary, felt the breeze that would convert itself into the tornado that became the French Revolution. He saw science and rationality as the solution to man's problems.

I wonder whether, during the 20 years when both Chesterfield and Franklin were living in London, they ever met. There is no record of such a meeting. If they had, what would they have talked about? Franklin did not want a break with England and Lord Chesterfield was very sympathetic with the claims of the colonies. Chesterfield died in 1773, before the American Revolution—an event he warned against, in a most civil tone. Franklin outlived him by 17 years.

Please forgive this discursive ramble, but I have been waiting for a time and place to talk about Lord Chesterfield and Benjamin Franklin and civility, like the man in Chesterfield's anecdote who had a compulsion to speak about guns.

Now on to civility and the law. The legal profession has produced an abundance of writing on civility, commenting on the need for civility, the lack of civility, the reasons for incivility, and even the need for a published code of civility.

The reasons for the lack of civility are: (1) the legal community is so large that the lawyers do not know each other anymore, and treat each other as strangers out to do harm to each other; (2) the stakes in litigation are much higher than they used to be, and clients cannot afford to lose and press their lawyers to do whatever is necessary to win; and (3) the tradition of civility that used to be transmitted to young lawyers is gone. Young lawyers jump around from firm to firm in search of career advantages. They do not stay in one firm long enough to find a worthwhile role model.

If these are the reasons the legal profession is becoming increasingly uncivil, how best to correct the problem? Many jurisdictions have adopted a written civility code for lawyers, but I question the value of such codes. I believe incivility at the trial bar is easily controlled by the trial judge. There are some judges who have no trouble with lawyers. Not only are the lawyers well behaved before these judges, the lawyers enjoy engaging in the traditional flattery that is expected of them when addressing the court.

There are other judges who are always in trouble with lawyers. Why is this? Lawyers quickly learn what a judge will put up with and which judges have such a sense of dignity that shameful conduct before such a judge is unthinkable. A judge who invariably shows up late to take the bench will find his or her courtroom lacking in civility. A judge who is unprepared will have civility problems. A judge who loses his or her temper, or who is undisciplined, will see lawyers acting in a similar manner.

Judging is a demanding occupation. It requires good manners, promptness in ruling, and the ability to listen to nonsense from lawyers and witnesses, without interruption. A judge must understand that the flattery of counsel directed toward the judge and occasionally flattery directed by the judge to counsel is mechanical rather than based on the merits. One observer has said that even an eighteenth-century gallant, seeking to persuade difficult lady to yield to his advances, would not abase himself as much as counsel does towards the judge. The words frequently used are:

"Your Honor has put it so much better than I can"; "Your Honor is, as always, very helpful"; "As Your Honor knows"; and, of course, the inevitable "If Your Honor pleases."

There was a local judge who enjoyed this two-way traffic in flattery. He might say to the defendant, "Mr. Jones, your lawyer has said everything that could possibly be said on your behalf. Your lawyer is one of the finest, most competent members of our bar." The lawyer might then respond, "Your Honor is very patient and sensitive to these delicate issues." This particular judge had two motives in mind when praising lawyers. He wanted to help the lawyer in the eyes of his client and he wanted to provide some spending money for the court reporter. When the praise of the lawyer is effusive the lawyer invariably orders a copy of the transcript from the court reporter—for which the court reporter charges five dollars a page.

There are, however, a few judges who appear to object to the tradition. This is a pity, for without the judge to guide the process, the tradition of civility is lost. When I was much younger, I was before one of these judges. He had the habit of saying to counsel, "Don't say 'As Your Honor knows.' Don't repeat 'If the court pleases.' It is a waste of time." I never used this type of mechanical flattery again before this judge—I never imputed to him the slightest knowledge of the law. And I never won a case in front of him.

30 GOLDEN RULES

Recently I participated in a series of long, drawn-out negotiations. There were periods when there was nothing to do but wait for responses to cell phone calls to principals hiding out, so it seemed, all over the world. After the third day I brought with me several books giving advice on how to negotiate.

These books contain common-sense observations on human nature that were known a thousand years ago, together with sociological studies of how people behave during a negotiation, and complicated mathematical formulae attempting to capture human cynicism and the techniques of used-car salesmen and stockbrokers in algebraic equations flecked with x's, and n's, and $E=mc^2$. I remain unconvinced that algebra can catch a liar.

During one of the breaks I asked co-counsel whether he reads books or attends courses in negotiation. He said he does not. He knew there was much to be learned, but his habits were formed by years of give-and-take, and it was too late for him to try and learn new tricks. I think that is where I am.

When I act as a mediator and one or both of the parties to the negotiation shows signs of having taken a course in the art of negotiation, I know I am in for trouble. The course shows through and slows things down. But things go rather well if I know the lawyers and they put aside technique. In a private meeting with each side, I often can get to the issues without the rain dance.

We are told lawyers must not engage in misrepresentation. But negotiation is of the marketplace with its exaggerations and disparagements. It is far away from solemn statements made under oath subject to the penalties of perjury.

George Washington, in his March 30, 1796, message to the House of Representatives, caught the spirit. Although he referred to foreign negotiations, what he said applies to many domestic negotiations:

> The nature of foreign negotiations requires caution, and their success must often depend on secrecy; and, even when brought to a conclusion, a full disclosure of all the measures, demands, or eventual concessions, which may have been proposed or contemplated, would be extremely impolitic; for this might have a pernicious influence on future negotiations, or produce immediate inconveniences, perhaps danger and mis-chief, in relation to other powers.

It has been said that a good negotiator must have the hide of an elephant. The patience of Job. The cunning of Machiavelli. A mask for a face. The resourcefulness of Casanova. The nerve of a bandit. And the concentration of a card cheat. On occasion I have had the feeling such a person was sitting across from me at the conference table.

We all learn the rules of the game by experience. Here are the thirty golden rules experience has taught me:

☞ Patience, patience, and more patience. Persistence, persistence, and more persistence.

☞ Don't negotiate in a hurry.

☞ If knowledge is power, you lose power when you talk and gain power when you listen. Be a dangerous listener. Don't interrupt.

☞ Get used to being told "no." Saying "no" often leads to getting to "yes."

☞ "No" may mean "maybe," "not at this time," "not exactly."

☞ At the conference table, don't be clever, be useful.

☞ Know when to suspend to let time bring a better setting.

☞ Avoid repeating your best points.

☞ Avoid having your client available at the table.

☞ Keep something in reserve. Your adversary may be doing just that.

☞ Once there is agreement on the main issues, immediately settle the details, including the precise language of the closing documents.

☞ Have an associate take notes.

☞ Have in mind what your next move is if the negotiation fails.

☞ Know what your adversary really wants: prestige, to look good to his principal, to get home before seven o'clock, to catch a plane, to delay so he will be better prepared at some later date?

☞ Identify what you can give away without affecting what you really want.

☛ Determine how payment is to be made: all cash, periodic payments, or personal guarantees?

☛ Use emotion only as a device. Separate yourself from the case. Indignation and sarcasm are to be used, if at all, with care.

☛ When a document is presented, read it line by line, noting the date, who received copies, and whether it refers to other writings. Is it the original?

☛ When the session is over, identify all your papers, and put them in order before leaving the room. Make sure that your adversary has none of your papers.

☛ What you say casually may be turned against you at a crucial time.

☛ "In the range of" means the lower figure.

☛ Don't correct every mistake of fact when asserted by your adversary. Reserve as many as you can for later use.

☛ Don't deal in absolutes. Beware of standing on principle.

☛ Patience, patience, patience.

☛ Make up your mind what you want before the negotiation begins.

☛ Don't be afraid of leaving something on the table.

☛ Although everything is off the record, nothing is off the record.

☛ When you obtain a concession, write it down. Don't ask that it be repeated. It will be modified.

☛ A bully is to be met with dignity and infinite resources of silence interrupted by an occasional undisputed fact.

☛ And, above all, not too much zeal and always patience, patience, and more patience. What's the rush?

CHARACTER AND REPUTATION

Thebe was a time when what is called character testimony was a good defense in a criminal case. Three or four witnesses testifying to the reputation of the defendant for truthfulness and honesty together with a rousing closing argument could bring in an acquittal. Such closing arguments picked up on the court's instruction that character testimony standing alone may create a reasonable doubt as to the defendant's guilt.

Here is the way the argument goes:

The court will instruct you that evidence of good character may, standing alone, create a reasonable doubt, a reasonable doubt that requires you to acquit the defendant. Ladies and Gentlemen of the jury, in some cases there is no other defense against prosecution witnesses who give perjured testimony. You have heard the character witnesses testify that my client is an

51

honorable and good man. His good character, established week by week, month by month, year by year, repels the allegation he suddenly repudiated a lifetime of honesty and became a criminal.

Although the witnesses were called character witnesses, they were in fact reputation witnesses whose testimony was restricted to what they knew of the general reputation of the defendant. The defendant's true character—what it really was—remained known only to the defendant. Mark Twain made the point when he said if a man's reputation was to meet on the street the man's true character, they would not recognize each other.

Despite the common-law restriction that a character witness was permitted only to say what others thought of the defendant (not what the witness himself thought of the defendant), a resourceful witness would always find a way to convey his own wonderful feelings about the defendant.

Theodore Roosevelt was such a witness. Roosevelt once appeared as a character witness for a prominent Washington banker charged with a felony related to bank records. Frank Hogan of Hogan & Hartson represented the banker. The trial took place in what is now called the old United States District Court Building at Fifth Street and Indiana Avenue.

In speeches made years later, Frank Hogan fondly recalled that when Teddy Roosevelt entered the courtroom everyone stood up. Then Roosevelt took over and gave in colorful language his own personal view that the defendant, although a banker, was a saint, all in violation of the applicable rules of evidence.

Then Roosevelt looked at the judge and said: "And by the way, Judge, I knew I had met you somewhere. I appointed you because of your civic righteousness, because of your interest in the poor of this city, on my committee to clean out the slums. That's what I did, and you were one of the best men on the committee I ever had. I know, Gentlemen of the jury, you are glad to hear that about your judge. I knew I recognized him."

When Roosevelt left the courtroom he passed in front of the jury on his way out. He said, "Goodbye, Gentlemen of the jury. I always like to appear before a jury of my fellow citizens, for you are rendering a public service. You are rendering a really great public service, just as much as the judge there. You are here to do justice. That's why you are here—and I know you are going to do it, I know you are going to do it." The jury did the right thing and Frank Hogan got his acquittal.

There is a school of thought that contends that a character witness who has had an opportunity to observe the defendant when off-guard, such as an employee of the defendant who saw him in good times and bad over a long period of time, has more credibility than a so-called face card witness.

There are a number of reasons why character testimony does not have the impact it once did. Firstly, a defendant nowadays often does not testify in his own behalf. The defendant is told by counsel that if he takes the stand and he is convicted, he may have substantially increased his sentence because the judge has reason to believe that the defendant lied under oath. Therefore, stay off the stand. Character testimony concerning the defendant's reputation for truthfulness and honesty is out of place when the defendant does not testify.

Another reason is that trials have changed. The prosecutor has evidentiary resources unavailable years ago. He has witnesses who have been granted immunity and who know more about the character of the defendant than any character witness the defendant may call.

The third reason and perhaps the most important is that the general view of human nature has changed. In early novels, the hero was all good and the villain was all bad. Charles Dickens's novels demonstrate the point. His main characters are either wonderfully wonderful or as bad as bad can be.

Gradually fictional characters changed. The hero is not all virtue and the villain is not all vice. We have changed also. We no longer believe in unflawed goodness. Somerset Maugham, the novelist, and a sophisticated observer of human nature, had this to say: "Selfishness and kindliness, idealism and sensuality, vanity, shyness, disinterestedness, courage, laziness, nervousness, obstinacy, and diffidence, they can all exist in a single person and form a plausible harmony."

Juries carry with them to the jury box this general skepticism. They know people who are generally good and who then decide to steal from their employer. They read of such cases every day in the papers and see them on TV every evening. Therefore jurors are more skeptical of character testimony than they were when life was simpler.

If we needed any additional corroboration, we are getting it from the historians who eagerly tell us that even the Founding Fathers—Washington, Adams, Jefferson, and Hamilton—had their bad days as well as their good days.

WORRY

> One of the principal functions of any lawyer anywhere is to worry;
> he has to worry about deadlines, about blunders, about thorough-
> ness of research, about that possible case not unearthed that can
> knock him off his pins.
>
> Roy A. Redfield

Lloyd Paul Stryker, the author of *The Art of Advocacy* (1954), is described on the cover of the book as a man whose clients included judges, district attorneys, political leaders, and prominent figures in the world of government, business, and society, and as one of New York's top-flight trial lawyers.

Despite Mr. Stryker's standing in the profession, he stated he had the constant worry of every practicing lawyer: I need a new, good case. Stryker said that even the most successful advocates have their long, dry spells. A constant lawyer's worry. When will I get a new, good case?

Another constant lawyer's worry is overhead. We are going through a period where overhead is equivalent to the Cold War armaments race. If a competitor buys new computers, we buy new computers. If a competitor puts in expensive oriental rugs, we put in expensive orientals. If the competitor puts in the malachite-top conference room table, we go malachite. Not to get ahead, but just to stay even. In a legal arms race, all we can do is stay even. It is the suppliers who profit.

Another constant worry is that of the associate who is waiting to see if she makes partner. Those who don't make partner can assuage despair by considering what is happening these days to new partners. The new partner learns that a partnership is defined as an agreement among partners to share not only profits but also losses. Therefore it is appropriate for the senior partners to inform the new partner of the threatened default of the bank loan and the threatened withdrawal of the firm's very profitable merger section. If the withdrawal takes place, it will be impossible to pay the rent. The new partner finds she has a whole set of new worries.

Each new case brings its unique worries, worries that come and go with the case. Is the client who sits before me one of those who will give me trouble? This client, in response to my request for documents, puts on the desk a stack of old letters held together by a rubber band. Each letter is stapled to its envelope. I grow apprehensive. Here are the telltale signs of persecution mania. Will each letter I send the client be stapled to the envelope for future use against me? Will I be part of the general conspiracy of people who claim they mailed letters when in fact no letter was mailed?

I take the letters, pull off the envelopes, and boldly throw the envelopes in the trash. As I do so, I tell the client about a lawyer I once worked for and how his persecution mania interfered with his competence. He wasted his client's money by pursuing shadows and false leads. I tell the client that I don't want a file cluttered up with envelopes. Although I have seen cases turn on what was in a letter, I have never seen a case that turned on the envelope. If the client does not leave during the envelope destruction ceremony (some have), the ceremony bonds the client and me. Now he understands we shall not waste our time discussing convoluted conspiracies in which the president of the United States, the FBI, and the CIA have joined to assist the plaintiff bank that wants the client to repay the loan.

Each case brings its own set of facts to worry about. I return to Mr. Stryker:

> The really difficult problem in the preparation of the case is to learn what the facts are, and no matter how long or conscientiously you work, you will never know them all. The law seldom decides the issue, the facts do; and as contrasted with the ascertainment of the facts, the law is relatively easy to discover. There are a hundred good researchers of the law to one who has a genius, I may say a nose, for the discovery of the true facts.

Not only do I need to get the facts, I need to organize them in a chronology. In time the chronology itself becomes a fact. It shows what is going on when an important action was taken. It discloses hidden motives. What were the financial pressures at the time? What was worrying the parties? What happened just before and just after the important events? Who wanted what and when? *Cherchez le* greed.

Occasionally a client appears with a problem that must be solved or the client is ruined. What to do? Each choice leads to new worries. Several separate lines of evil are ready to pounce and at the same time. But I also know that evil as well as good is unpunctual and often fails to keep its appointments. And I find that a discussion with another lawyer is comforting. In such discussions I often learn I missed an essential point in the analysis. My concentration on one issue blinded me to another. After a sufficient period of worry, things mature in the mind and one choice appears better than others. It is acted on. Then another set of choices appears and the cycle repeats itself.

I have noticed that when the worries pile up they are dispelled by taking action. Action starts up excitement. I make a new action list and I get to work, checking off item by item. I keep repeating to myself that a person who does not worry is unfit for the practice of law. The lawyer's function is to worry and to get paid for it. That's the deal, so don't worry about it.

DEFAMATION

Afriend was in the office sounding me out about a lawsuit against his boss. His bully of a boss had called him a liar in front of some important people. Didn't I think this was an actionable case of defamation?

At any given time there are people who wish to fight back against a boss or a neighbor or a business associate because of something nasty the person said or wrote. The victim wants to sue for defamation. (A word about terminology: *defamation* is the general term that includes both libel and slander. Libel written, slander spoken.)

As he spoke I had in mind the cautionary proverb that a person who sues because somebody calls him a liar may find that a jury believes he *is* in fact a liar.

I asked what his boss's salary was. It was a good salary, but not enough for the boss to pay a substantial judgment—and the expense of defamation litigation requires a substantial judgment to justify the time and expense on a contingent-fee basis. Working people can't afford to pay by the hour for defamation litigation. It's too expensive. Defamation law is unsettled, and unsettled law triggers pleadings, motions, and papers.

No, a lawsuit wasn't the solution to my friend's problem. I spoke of how one wise lawyer dealt with a similar situation. He sent a letter to the slanderer stating that the matter was under careful investigation. The letter would trigger the paranoia of the slanderer. He himself was now under investigation. He had better watch what he said. He may be sued. Most of the time, the defamer defamed no more.

Rarely does a really good defamation case walk in the door. Here are the criteria. The defamatory statement must be demonstrably false and made with the intent to injure. The defamatory statement must have caused a provable loss of income in addition to claims of injury to reputation. And finally, the defendant must have lots of money to pay a judgment.

The facts provided by the clients who want to sue often meet two of the requirements, but rarely all three. Few potential plaintiffs can prove a loss of income caused by the defamation. The friends of the defamed person do not believe the lies, and his enemies already believe them. A proximate cause issue.

Some defamation cases are brought not because the case is a good one but because something must be done to show indignation. This is especially true when the dispute has political overtones. Politicians commence defamation suits to express outrage, thereby demonstrating their own purity. Just as the alleged libel may be believed by some because it has appeared in print, a denial coupled with a lawsuit may similarly convince some that the libel is untrue. The litigants, once out of public eye, may give occasional press interviews denouncing the other, but the lawsuit goes on the stet docket, probably never to be tried. Occasionally the plaintiff's cheerleaders convince the plaintiff to go to trial. The trial can prove a disaster. General William Westmoreland's case against CBS is one example.

One of the big-name plaintiffs in a defamation suit that never went to trial was General Douglas MacArthur. In 1943 the general sued the *Washington Times-Herald* and its columnist Drew Pearson for libel. The paper accused the general of proposing 19-gun salutes for friends and "pulling wires" to further his ambition. The general wanted $750,000 as fair compensation for injury to his reputation. The case was never tried.

While it was pending, there was a knock on the door of Pearson's Georgetown residence—fate had sent Pearson a perfect defense, in the form of a beautiful Eurasian woman. She had bolted from the Chastleton Apartments at 16th and R streets, N.W., where she had been sequestered by the general. She placed in Pearson's hands a collection of General MacArthur's love letters to her. Shortly thereafter the general was made aware that Drew Pearson possessed some interesting documents the general might not want to see in print. MacArthur dropped his lawsuit, and the letters were never published.

In 1957 General Harry Vaughan, President Truman's military aide from 1945 to 1953, was provoked into filing a defamation suit against the *Saturday Evening Post*. At the time, the *Post* was trying to boost circulation with sensational articles. The November 3, 1956, article about Vaughan identified people who were sent to jail because of Drew Pearson's local newspaper columns. Next to it was a picture of General Vaughan testifying at a public hearing. The caption read, "Many Pearson charges against Harry Vaughan were later confirmed by testimony before Senate Committee." Vaughan and others read the caption and the photograph as charging Vaughan with dishonesty.

Fed up with Pearson and with the *Post,* Vaughan decided not only to file suit but also to risk a trial. The *Post* wished the jury to believe that Vaughan was mixed up with five-percenters and was a tool of lobbyists. At trial, Vaughan was questioned at length about instances that the *Post* hoped would show him as a corrupt influence-peddler. Unimpressed by the *Post*'s defense, the jury returned a $10,000 verdict for Vaughan for damage to his reputation. It did not, however, award punitive damages.

The verdict was a disappointment to Vaughan's lawyers, but not to Vaughan. It gave him bragging privileges. He was a man who saw it through to a difficult but exculpatory end.

Two plaintiffs who commenced defamation suits discovered that the defamation suit can take a bad turn. Although they were plaintiffs in the civil suit, they ended up as defendants in criminal prosecutions, and both were convicted. Their names? Alger Hiss and Oscar Wilde.

MADAM ROSA

Thank here is a fortune-teller's shop on Connecticut Avenue, and when I walk by it several thoughts come to mind. First, my wonderment that people still believe in fortune-telling, clairvoyance, palmistry, psychic powers, and astrology in these days of scorching skepticism. Second, I think once again of Joseph Duvall (that is not his real name). Joseph looked like he was somebody: He was tall and well-dressed, and he spoke in the authoritative tones of a politician. He had been elected to various offices in his hometown before he decided to practice law here in Washington. When we worked on cases together, I learned that Joseph's main source of business was Madam Rosa, an astrologer/fortune-teller. She sent him more legal work than he could handle. Much of it involved the problems of elderly people proud to say their wealth was based on Madam Rosa's advice.

If a case that Madam Rosa power-steered to Joseph ended up in court, Madam Rosa conducted a pretrial conference/focus group in her chambers. The usual props were there, incense, the crystal ball, the cards, the other bric-a-brac of the trade. I would not have been surprised to see a law book, perhaps *Dobbs on Remedies* or somebody on *Future Interests*. Joseph presented the facts and law. Thereafter Madam Rosa asked questions and then gave her opinion on whether to settle or go to trial. She had a good record. The cases she sent to trial were winners. She was especially gifted in predicting the high/low verdict range in cases against target defendants like the transit company.

Joseph said he met Madam Rosa when she appeared in his office one day with a problem concerning her storefront lease. When he asked who recommended him, she said he was recommended by the position of the stars.

Joseph liked to tell this story. He was representing a fortune-teller friend of Madam Rosa's charged with driving while drunk. A police reporter friend of Joseph's spotted him in court and asked what his case of the day was all about. Joseph said he was representing a fortune-teller. Joseph then said the judge would knock the case down from driving while under the influence to reckless driving and fine the woman fifty dollars. The reporter asked Joseph if that was what the fortune-teller predicted. Not only was that what she predicted, Joseph said he would bet ten dollars on it. Joseph appeared with his client and the judge did reduce the charge to reckless driving but fined the client only twenty-five dollars. Joseph stood up at his client's urging and said, "Judge, can you make that fifty dollars?"

Joseph divided fortune-tellers into the true believers and the competent frauds. The true believers sincerely believe they have the gift. They take themselves seriously. One of them explained the gift this way. Evolution gave to the animal kingdom a lot of instinct and little intelligence. A lot of instinct can do things that intelligence can never do. A very small, vulnerable butterfly by instinct finds its way year after year from Canada to an isolated spot in Mexico, a navigational feat beyond human comprehension. In such a flight the butterfly, flying only by instinct, makes thousands of computations concerning weather, wind, smoke, and changes in forestry that human intelligence could never do.

Evolution gave humans a lot of intelligence and little instinct. Intelligence involves comparison, analysis, induction, and deduction. It takes intelligence hours, days, years to figure out what intuition does in a flash. In rare cases a human is born with animal-like instinct that carries with it knowledge beyond intelligence, beyond cause and effect. It is this that explains the fortune-telling gift.

The true believer can be dangerous. He does not hesitate to predict misfortune or sudden death. The competent fraud does not have the intuitive gift. He picks up clues from the customer that make it appear that he knows things about the customer that could only come through some mysterious power. I have worked with lawyers who have this talent in selecting jurors and in conducting a cross-examination.

The competent fraud makes no dire predictions. He gives a balanced view of life's ups and downs, falling in love, falling out of love, and the possibility of inherited wealth.

Joseph said that the high-profile true believers and the competent frauds, both of them, have something in common—they vote the straight Republican ticket. Joseph's political sophistication and the popularity of Jean Dixon, the well-known astrologer in the 1950's and 1960's, corroborated his statement. Jean Dixon did a good business during the presidential election years predicting comfortable margins for Nixon and Eisenhower.

Perhaps the reason high-profile astrologers tend to vote Republican is that they take their cue from their up-market clientele. It may be what a Madam Rosa has on offer does not attract liberal intellectuals who contend their beliefs are always entirely high-minded, virtuous, and reasonable and therefore uninfluenced by abracadabra.

My reaction to fortune-tellers is negative simply because I don't want to know what's next. Although the predictions of most psychics, fortune-tellers, clairvoyants, tarot card readers, and palmists are harmless, I am apprehensive that I may run into a true believer who will predict bad news ahead. Therefore I am never tempted to have a Madam Rosa give me a reading. The French writer Alain says it very well:

> I know someone who showed his palm to a fortune-teller in order to know his future. He told me he did it just for fun, and didn't really believe in it. Even so, I would have advised him against it, if he had asked me, because it is a dangerous way to have fun. It is very easy not to believe, as long as nothing has yet been said; for then there is nothing for you or anyone else to believe. Disbelief is easy at the outset, but soon becomes difficult; fortune-tellers know this very well. "If you don't believe in it," they say, "what are you afraid of?" And thus the trap is set. As for me, I am afraid of believing, for who knows what they will tell me.

There you have it.

CLIENTS

You cannot practice law without
them. You cannot establish independence in a law firm these wonderful days without a group of clients who will follow you from
firm to firm.

There are two main categories of clients: the client who pays
a reasonable bill when rendered and the client who does not.
Those who pay and accompany their payment with a letter of
thanks are the rare species.

The dominant species is the client who turns belligerent
when the time comes to pay. He is all for litigation, no matter the
cost, until the computer clicks out the bill. Then all that the lawyer
was encouraged to do to get at the adversary is called into question. Why so many depositions? Why so many motions? The terms
of engagement now change. The lawyer is the adversary.

The ups and downs of the real estate market brought into
existence another client type, the underfunded commercial litiga-

tor. He wants to litigate his deals for whatever advantages litigation produces. He wants to be in the game, so to speak. He sees the big players litigating each deal in order to get a better deal. It is he who thought up the concept of lender liability. No lawyer, on his own, would have the imagination to create a cause of action against a lender because the lender has the audacity to want to be paid as promised.

The underfunded commercial litigator puts up just enough money to pay the retainer, the entrance fee. His lawyer files the original pleadings—the complaint or the answer and obligatory counterclaim. In a few discovery waves the retainer is used up. By this time the lawyer and the client are litigation friends. They dine together and the client puts it on his credit card. They may take vacations together. The lawyer is in the process of being manipulated just the way the client manipulated those involved in the real estate deal that is the subject of the pending litigation.

What makes the arrangement particularly onerous for the lawyer is the client's rejection of the settlement offer that would provide a little money for the client and would pay the lawyer's bills. The client's strategy is to push the issue to the point where the lawyer begs the client to settle. The client then says, "But why should I settle? You get paid but what is in it for me? Reduce your bill and we can do some business." The trap is sprung.

I have often wondered why it is that lawyers take on clients known within the profession to be slow-pay or no-pay. Perhaps the lawyer who signs on believes he can outfox the client. He is wrong. The client does not have to play by any rules. The lawyer does. The lawyer loses. Well, maybe not always. There is a story concerning Max Steuer, a leading New York trial lawyer in the 1920's and 1930's. He was involved in an arbitration hearing. He represented a client interested in overzealous representation and underpaid legal services. Steuer said not a word at the hearing until a white envelope passed from the client to Steuer's co-counsel, who made a count of the cash. When co-counsel nodded, Steuer announced he was ready.

The client I find interesting is the one who interviews lawyers before committing. He says his case is a sure thing. There are five lawyers bidding for the case. One letter and there will be a huge settlement. Experience has taught me to tell such a client that I do not accept sure things. I have never had a sure thing. I would not know how to deal with a sure thing. The client should consult a sure-thing specialist.

And what of the client who quivers with suspicion concerning everything and everybody? I enjoy spending time with such people, not because I wish to represent them but to study the symptoms of an incurable disorder. Such a person is hesitant to tell me the facts because I might have as a client the person he wishes to sue. He is reluctant to show me the documents for fear I may misplace them. My pleasure is in taking all the letters with the envelopes attached. I tear off the envelopes and toss them into the trash as I pronounce that in over forty years of practice I have never seen a case where the envelope was of any evidentiary importance. I have had the potential client run over to the trash basket, retrieve the envelopes, and flee the office.

The wish to litigate, for some people, can be an obsession. Piero Calamandrei, in his book *Eulogy of Judges*, describes such a person.

> I know a venerable litigant, now more than ninety
> years old, who after the age of sixty brought a suit over
> a disputed inheritance. His adversaries, who were then

young, thought the best tactics were to wear the old man out by dilatory methods in order to hasten his death, which they expected in the near future. Thus began an epic duel between Civil procedure and longevity. As the years have passed generations of lawyers have defended the parties, and one by one the judges who handed down the early decisions have gone to their last rest. The old gentleman, instead of aging, seems to take on new life from every procedural objection which further postpones the final decision.

I have met and represented the type. At heart he is a born gambler. Lawsuits and the lottery are his source of stimulation. Gambler that he is, he would rather lose a lawsuit than not to be in litigation at all. And there is always the appeal.

HOW TO GET A
CONFESSION

T here is talk now of using truth serum to get the truth from a terrorist. Does truth serum work? Who knows? There is also talk of using the tried-and-true method of getting confessions—moderately severe torture.

This brings to mind the apocryphal remark of the Calcutta policeman who said rubbing red pepper into the eyes of the poor devil until he confesses is more efficient than looking for witnesses in the noonday sun. Mad dogs and Englishmen and all that.

The law is skeptical of confessions made outside the court-room. People may confess for reasons known and unknown and be innocent. The temptation to extort confessions is strong. Unless it is resisted it will push out the traditional means of getting the evidence. The balance in our legal system that discourages the use of questionable means is a delicate adjustment. "Take but degree away. Untune that string, and hark! What discord follows."

In the 1940s Fred E. Inbau (1909–1998), of Northwestern University Criminal Law Department, was fascinated by and wrote frequently on the subject of criminal interrogation. His book, *Criminal Interrogation and Confessions,* urged the police to use any kind of artifice, deception, and trick to get a confession. According to Inbau, anything goes. Inbau was before the Miranda warning.

There is a story that has been told of a Chicago criminal lawyer who knew Inbau and his techniques and who went Inbau one better.

We shall call the criminal lawyer Fred Bellows. His son, Cliff Bellows, was killed in an elevator accident. Cliff was in an office building elevator with five other passengers. The elevator went out of control and took a free fall from the tenth floor to the basement. The passengers were badly injured and were trapped for six hours before the rescue team hammered and drilled through the elevator top and freed them. Cliff was found dead. It was assumed the cause of death was his severe injuries. However, the autopsy disclosed something strange. Cliff Bellows had a bullet in his heart.

The police learned that Cliff carried a gun because of threats made against his criminal-lawyer father. Thereafter the police declared that Cliff's death was a suicide. Cliff was so badly injured he decided, so it was thought, that if he survived life would not be worth living. He must have shot himself with his own gun. The fact that the others in the elevator were unaware of the gunshot was explained by the hammering and banging by the rescue crew.

Cliff's father had trouble with the way the police closed the case as a suicide. Cliff was not the type to commit suicide. Mr. Bellows decided to conduct his own investigation.

He learned that one of the persons on the elevator could have known Cliff because they worked for the same company and they may have gotten on at different floors. Bellows discovered evidence that pointed to a particular person on the elevator who may have had a motive to kill Cliff based on disagreements at the brokerage firm where they worked. But the evidence was weak, certainly not strong enough to interest a prosecutor. Bellows needed a confession.

A year after Cliff's death Mr. Bellows invited the occupants of the elevator to his home for dinner. The invitation said each would learn something new about the elevator accident.

On the evening in question they all showed up. Dinner was served promptly. After dinner Mr. Bellows said to the group that he was skeptical that his son committed suicide. He believed Cliff was killed by his own gun, but the gun was used by somebody else who was in the elevator.

"The person who killed my son is now in this room. That person has been served a meal different than the meal that was served to the others. His meal and his alone contained poison. A poison that takes effect in 10 minutes."

Bellows then said, "He knows who he is. He is free to leave the room right now, and my chauffeur will take him to the hospital in time to save his life. If he doesn't want to leave, he can save himself by eating from the bowl of custard dessert that is now being placed in the center of the table. The dessert contains the antidote to the poison that was in the meal. But he must act quickly."

One of the persons had been drinking too much. He made fun of the whole ceremony. He said it was like an old 1930's movie that he had seen or maybe a Sherlock Holmes story he'd read.

When nobody else took any of the dessert, he scooped out a generous portion and ate it.

Bellows said to him: "Sir, you waited too long. I don't think the antidote will work."

The person who had eaten the dessert looked startled, and then collapsed. In a few minutes he was unconscious.

Bellows said to the group,

Gentlemen, I deceived you. When I said there was poison in the dinner of the person I suspected of murdering my son, I was lying. And when I said that the dessert contained the antidote to the poison, of course that was a lie.

Then you may ask why this man is stretched out unconscious on the floor. It is because the dessert did have something in it. Not an antidote but a strong soporific. He is sleeping and in time he will wake up.

I tricked him into giving what in law is called an implied confession. It is a confession implied by the circumstances. My case against him has moved from the speculative to the presumptive.

I don't want to leave it there. When he gets up you will see a demonstration of the art of cross-examination. Now that I have this implied confession, I will work backwards to get at the motive. That is what interests me. Why did he murder my son?

While we wait for the subject of our inquiry to wake up, let's have some dessert, some dessert that I will eat with you. How about chocolate cheesecake? I will eat the first slice.

PAWNSHOPS, PEARLS,
AND BASIC BLACK

What to do with old law school casebooks? They remain on the shelf, unopened, despite the fact that they take up needed space. Such books have nostalgic staying power. Nevertheless, the time comes when they must be taken down and put in a box for storage in the garage with instructions to your executor to throw them out.

While acting on my own advice and putting the books away, my Personal Property casebook, dark blue, heavy, and bruised, caught my eye because of a bookmark at *Easterly v. Horning*, 30 U.S. App. D.C. 225, decided in 1908. The case deals with a dispute involving title to personal property. The defendant, George D. Horning, operated a Washington pawnshop. The plaintiff, Easterly, alleged that Mr. Horning should have known that the woman who pawned jewelry with Mr. Horning was not the true owner of the jewelry. She wanted the jewelry back. Horning, who lent $300 against the jewelry as security, defended by saying he was a "bona fide pawnee for value."

The Horning pawnshop was still in business up to a few years ago. It had moved long ago from downtown Washington to Rosslyn, Virginia, as the pawnshops found northern Virginia a more hospitable place. The Horning pawnshop recently closed down in favor of renting the space to a restaurant that is utilizing the pawnshop memorabilia.

In the 1940's there were pawnshops huddled around Ninth and E streets. Two of them disappeared to make way for the FBI building. The window display of these shops was intriguing. Saxophones, clarinets, accordions, banjos, guitars, portable typewriters, trays of fraternity and class rings, cuff links, studs, diamond rings, ruby rings, rhinestone rings, bracelets, antique medals, electric razors, clocks, watches, radios, phonographs, and silver photo frames.

The merchandise on display came into the pawnshop as security for a much needed loan that was to be redeemed at a fixed date by bringing in the pawn ticket and paying the loan and paying the additional strong interest rate. If the borrower defaulted, the security became the property of the pawnshop. As stated in *Easterly*, the pawnshop owner became a bona fide pawnee for value.

Why do people resort to pawnshops that charge such a high rate of interest? Banks will not make quick loans secured by used musical instruments. Banks want unencumbered real estate. The friendly port of call for those in need of cash right away is the local pawnbroker.

Pawnshops have been around a long time to fill this need. One commentator sums it up this way: "If we desire to trace with minuteness the history of pawnbroking, we must go back to the earliest ages of the world, since the business of lending money on portable security is one of the most ancient of human occupations."

It takes real talent to run a pawnshop. The two ways of making money—having the borrower pay off the loan with interest or having the borrower default and then selling the security at a profit—must be balanced against the ways of losing money. The pawnbroker loses if he lends more than the security is worth. This requires a knowledge of the market value of portable security. The pawnbroker must be an expert on the value of jewelry, musical instruments, luggage, and many other things that I saw in the pawnshop windows near Ninth and E streets.

Pawnbrokers must also be on the alert to make sure that the person who brings in the goods is the real owner. If the pawnbroker does not get good title, he has no legal right to keep the security that covers the loan. Most states require the pawnbroker to report to the police every item that is pawned. This gives the police a check on efforts by thieves to dispose of stolen goods.

Pawnbrokers show up in novels and movies. There are the novels in which the hero, a talented but unsuccessful writer, runs out of money. He takes his typewriter to the pawnshop to get money to buy food and drink. Just days before he will lose the typewriter unless he pays up, he gets a letter from a publisher who wants to buy the manuscript. In the movie *The Lost Week-End*, Ray Milland, playing the role of an alcoholic writer, is a frequent visitor to the corner pawnshop. Dostoyevsky's *Crime and Punishment* turns on Raskolnikov's murder of a woman who runs the pawnshop.

The chance finding of a lost pawn ticket provides a handy literary device. Try this:

A rich-too-quick Wall Street broker—we'll call him J. P. Leverage—is carrying on a love affair with another rich-too-quick broker's wife. J. P. makes a killing on the stock market. He decides to celebrate by buying his girlfriend a beautiful pearl necklace.

When he presents it to her, and after the oohs and ahs, she asks how she will explain this to her insanely jealous husband. J. P. says to tell him it's a fake. She says it won't work, her husband has a jeweler's eye.

J. P. has a backup plan. "We'll go to the pawnshop, pawn the necklace, and you'll take the pawn ticket to your husband and tell him you found it and you want him to redeem it." She follows orders.

Two days later her husband calls her at home and tells her to drop by his office. He has been to the pawnbroker. She will like what he got.

She puts on the basic black dress that sets off the pearls and goes to the office. Her husband shows her two silver candlesticks. "Aren't these beautiful? Somebody must have really needed money to pawn these." He then calls to his secretary and says, "My wife and I are going to dinner. Would you wrap the candlesticks that are in the front room and have them sent to my house."

The secretary walks into the room and says, "I certainly will." She is wearing a beautiful string of matched pearls.

THE INVESTMENT
BUILDING

The northwest corner of 15th and K streets is where the grand old Investment Building was located. I say "was located" because all that now remains of this once proud building are its exterior walls preserved for historical interest. A big sign hangs from the builder's rigging announcing that when the restoration is complete in August, 2001, Sidley & Austin will be the headline tenant.

I wonder whether Mr. Sidley and Mr. Austin believe in ghosts. I do, because when I walk over to the Investment Building to watch the progress of the rebuilding I see the ghosts of those who were tenants in the late 1940's and early 1950's. I see busy lawyers gathered around a conference table to discuss the need to allege contributory negligence in every Answer and the need of every Complaint to allege an extortionate *ad damnum* clause.

I see Frank Stoutenburg's drugstore with its lunch counter and tables and Rothschild's Cafeteria. They served as the building's club rooms. There, the boys (and in those days it was just boys) met and gave each other legal advice based on an in-depth knowledge of the relevant headnotes and what somebody told them. They spoke of their wins and losses and the big one that got away.

I see Harry LaPorte (not his real name) sitting at one of Stoutenburg's tables describing a supernatural event. LaPorte represented aggressive real estate speculators who believed in the divine right of caveat emptor. LaPorte, himself, was gentle and virtuous. As fate would have it, LaPorte often was in court defending the indefensible. Now the supernatural event. One of his clients was sued concerning a questionable business transaction. On cross-examination the client got caught by documents that contradicted his testimony on direct. His face reddened. He grabbed his chest, fell forward and died, right then and there, of a heart attack. Right there on the witness stand.

This restored LaPorte's faith in the human experiment. Who would have thought that a higher power would find its way to a courtroom where a witness was trying to lie his way around Exhibits 105 and 226 in Prince George's County Circuit Court. And who would have expected that the higher power would impose sentence within ten minutes of the crime. Life should be that way but rarely is.

LaPorte, when telling the story (and he told it many times), concluded the narration by saying "it happened once and maybe it will happen again." But the story does not end there. LaPorte was named the executor of the will of the deceased gentleman. In that role LaPorte cancelled the usurious notes that were part of the estate. This made many borrowers very happy. LaPorte's fees as executor freed him up from the trial work he detested.

I see Albert Beasley, a southern gentleman, patient, careful, and redundantly loquacious. Beasley represented casualty insurance carriers. His expertise was not in negotiating a good settlement for the carrier. No, he was the expert in drafting the release that closed the case. A big case or a small case, once concluded, must be honored with colorful language that gave protection against any contingency and "any and all persons, firms, and corporations, whether herein named or referred to or not, their respective heirs, legal representatives, successors, and assigns, of and from any and all causes of action, claims, demands, damages, costs, loss of services, expenses, compensation, and all consequential damages on account of, or in any way growing out of, any and all known and unknown personal injuries, death, and property damage resulting or to result from anything that happened from the beginning of the world to the date of execution. ..."

The Investment Building lawyers did not take themselves seriously as lawyers do today. They had no expectations of obtaining great wealth by practicing law. They were happy if they made ends meet with enough left over to make small investments in real estate ventures. The practice was local. Controversies among local businessmen, landlord and tenant cases, automobile accidents, the exploitation of the complicated probate law and procedure, the buying and selling of a small business, a dispute over a broker's commission, a suit to rescind a lifelong contract for dancing lessons, and domestic relations cases. Few ever handled a criminal case. That was for the lawyers on Fifth Street, not 15th Street.

The Investment Building's leading trial lawyer was H. Mason Welch. He, his brother Harry, and their friends, Jack Daley and Joe Barse, completed the firm. I called Joe to get his recollections of Mason Welch. Joe recalled Welch's astonishing memory and his speed in getting at the heart of the matter. These two qualities seem to be what a successful trial lawyer must have to excel.

Mason Welch, during a trial, took few notes. Nevertheless, he had instant recall of all the testimony. If you were to put Mason Welch's name in a Lexis search you would see that he appeared for the defendant doctor in just about every medical malpractice case tried during the time Welch practiced.

Occasionally a lawyer would make a big score. How did he spend the money? He would go to D'elia and Marks, custom tailors, on the second floor of the building, select the cloth and then watch as Marks made dozens of measurements and announced the measurements to D'elia—sleeve length, chest, low right shoulder, raised left hip.

If there was any money left after D'elia and Marks computed the bill, the lucky lawyer would treat himself to a shave in the Investment Building barbershop. A real shave by a real barber who knew how to apply hot towels and then the lather and then the quick ballet movements with the straight razor, a flick here and a flick there and then some stropping on the leather belt attached to the chair. The barber shop was on the 15th Street side with a big window facing the sidewalk. Passersby stopped to watch the show.

If Mr. Sidley and Mr. Austin see any ghosts I hope they give me a call so I can come right over. Perhaps Cam Burton will make an appearance. A good lawyer and a very good tap dancer practicing the "Puttin' on the Ritz" number, right there in his third-floor office.

THE TRIAL THAT
NEVER WAS

I am back in the courtroom. We have just settled the case in the judge's chambers. The judge, before dismissing the jury panel, says to the jurors: "While you have been waiting here, the lawyers in the case have been with me in chambers discussing the case, and the lawyers have reached a settlement. Courts encourage settlements. This settlement came about in part because you jurors were waiting in the courtroom. The presence of jurors encourages the lawyers to focus on the issues. The court and counsel thank you for your time and patience. Please report back to the jury room and you will be told if you are released for the day."

The judge made an interesting comment to me after the case settled: "Now that this case is settled, you have to worry about getting another case. I don't have to do that. I get all the cases I want from the assignment office."

How right she was. No worry about clients. No sending out bills.

Was it a good settlement or a bad settlement? Who won, who lost? Did I leave something on the table? Why, in the settlement discussion, didn't the defendants bring up that weak spot in our case—the causation issue? Were they holding back? During the negotiation in chambers did I say too much? Have I finally learned the eloquence of silence?

And what of the judge? Although she gave no indication of what her ruling would be, she did have *99 F.2d* on her desk. Was she going to follow it or distinguish it?

Would the judge have let us use the graphics in the opening statement?

What of the expert we identified after discovery closed? Would the judge have let us call him as a rebuttal witness?

What of the impeachment documents we intended to use on cross-examination? Would they have been excluded because we did not disclose them in discovery? But if we disclosed them, the defendant would have explained them away. Nothing like surprise. This judge had years of trial experience before she went on the bench. Would she understand our strategy and let us use them?

Is it a mistake to settle such a good case—good liability and good damages? Aren't these the cases to try? But as the judge told us in chambers, no case is perfect, and the defendant's offer made the case too dangerous to try. Yet there is a quality of recklessness— real or theatrical—that is a factor in a negotiation and in the trial practice itself.

When I arrived at court this morning and unpacked my five briefcases, I discovered I was missing the folder with the notes for the opening statement. I left them on my desk in the office. Why does this happen over and over again? When I prepare to go to court, an invisible adversary enters the office and hides the pleading file, my fountain pen, and the key exhibits.

I did remember to bring the draft of what was to be the great closing argument. As I read it through, I wonder how really great it would have been. A judge told me that juries fasten on to the court's instruction. His advice was to tailor the closing argument to the instructions and then praise the trial judge. He said it was a foolproof combination. I was going to try it out.

Perhaps I would have made a better argument if I had put aside these notes and relied on spontaneous inspiration. I have been lucky in having things come to mind while speaking. When I get one of these inspirational thoughts, I say it only once. I have learned not to repeat it. That is a dead giveaway. If I repeat the thought, I signal that the thought just occurred to me. And if it did just occur to me and it really has some validity, why did I not think of it long ago?

These bright ideas are of a type that students of closing arguments classify as romantic. Not classic. Romantic. Classic is preparation, orderliness, analysis, measurement, verifiable truth, scientific proof, deductive logic. Romantic is poetry, the unanalyzable, the imponderable, the intuitive, the mysterious, the emotional. It is the fleeting present, the glorious past, and the infinite possibilities of the future. It is melodrama and farce. It is the beauty that never was. It is the happy ending overcoming adversity. It is Charlie Chaplin mixing farce with tragedy. It is the big idea that cannot be bothered with details.

When the inspiration is in full tide, it discloses unexpected connections between the facts and the law that turn the case my way. These tricks are best done on rebuttal when the defendant's lawyer has no chance to reply.

Reliance on romantic inspiration is seductive. It requires no preparation, no work. It either happens or it doesn't. It is mysterious and irrational. There are those who believe in both inspiration and preparation. There are those who claim that preparation brings inspiration. Those are the winners.

After I settle a case I conduct the trial in my mind in the form of an elaborate daydream. I do all the things I am told to do at the continuing legal education conferences. I control the courtroom (whatever that means). I make objections that are short, to the point, and by the federal rule number. When my opponent tries to do the same, he misses the number and I correct him. The jury returns a verdict twice the size of the *ad damnum*. The verdict sticks because I amend the complaint in accordance with applicable federal rule.

Sara Teasdale, a poet who never tried a case, knew exactly what it's like:

It was a spring that never came,
But we have lived long enough to know
What we have never had, remains;
It is the things we have that go.

TIMING IS EVERYTHING

To every thing there is a season, and a time to every purpose under the heaven: / A time to be born, and a time to die; a time to plant, and a time to pluck up that which is planted; / A time to kill, and a time to heal; a time to break down, and a time to build up; / A time to weep, and a time to laugh; a time to mourn, and a time to dance; / A time to cast away stones, and a time to gather stones together; a time to embrace, and a time to refrain from embracing; / A time to get, and a time to lose; a time to keep, and a time to cast away; / A time to rend, and a time to sew; a time to keep silence, and a time to speak; / A time to love, and a time to hate; a time of war, and a time of peace.

Ecclesiastes 3:1-8

There is a time to sue, and there is a time to counterclaim. There is a time to add a defendant, and there is a time to drop a defendant. There is a time to admit, and there is a time to deny. There is a time to depose, and there is a time to use interrogatories. There is a time to speak, and there is a time to remain silent. There is a time to send a bill, and there is a time to reduce a bill. There is a time to be bold, and there is a time to be cautious. There is a time to cross-examine, and there is a time to waive.

There is a time to stay, and there is a time to leave. There is a time to form a partnership, and there is a time to dissolve a partnership. There is a time to persist, and there is a time to back off. There is a time to be reticent, and there is a time to tell all. There is a time for great things, and there is a time for small things.

There is a time to be prudent, and there is a time to be reckless. There is a time to ask for a raise, and there is a time not to ask for a raise. There is a time to sign a bank loan, and there is a time to cut overhead. There is a time to move to recuse the judge, and there is a time to flatter the judge. There is a time to go with a big law firm in order to pay the college loans, and there is a time to go straight.

There are people who are out of time with the times. There are those who are prematurely wise and who only come into their own time as they grow older. And there are those who are in time when young and out of time as they grow older. The right time for the right person at the right time.

And there are those who are persons for all seasons, such as Thomas More. And there are those who are in time no matter the time, such as Lord Rawlinson, a World War I general as described by Winston Churchill:

> During these vicissitudes he was always the same. In the best of fortunes or the worst, in the most dangerous and hopeless position or on the crest of the wave, he was always the same tough, cheery gentleman and sportsman. He had always the same welcome for a

friend, be he highly or lowly placed, and the same keen, practical, resolute outlook on facts however they might be marshalled.

Timing is everything in the performing arts. A pause at just the right time says more than any words can say. Jack Benny, the gifted comedian, made use of the pregnant pause. Benny's stage character was stingy. In one of his sketches a burglar holds a gun on Jack Benny and says, "Your money or your life." The long pause. And then Benny says indignantly, "I'm thinking, I'm thinking."

Timing may be everything in the practice of law. As a preliminary matter, in deciding what to do for the client, one must consider whether it is the time for action or whether it is the time to do nothing. To let things be. Let sleeping dogs lie. This brings in the Precautionary Principle. Obedience to the principle requires that we do nothing unless the proponent of doing something can demonstrate by clear and convincing evidence that doing something will not make things worse.

The Precautionary Principle carries with it the temptation to procrastinate. Lawyers are addicted to procrastination. How do you determine whether you are using good judgment in leaving things as they are rather than putting off any decision? If the factors are considered and a decision is made, then you may not be procrastinating. But in my own case I am never sure.

Timing is of critical importance where the sentencing guidelines connect with the future of your client. The guidelines give the prosecutor the option to reduce the sentence by his filing a sentencing statement with the court declaring that the defendant has cooperated. Therefore a defense lawyer must not waste time in telling his client that there is no time to waste in offering cooperation to the prosecutor. If the client delays, he will find that the prosecutor has all the cooperation he needs from those who got there just in time.

A judge recently made this observation: "Counsel's ability to persuade the judge or jury is now far less important than his ability to persuade the prosecutor that the defendant should be allowed to cooperate with the government. ..." It is a race to the swift.

In a negotiation one must determine when it is time to hold and when it is time to fold. There are those who are content to leave something on the table in order to get, with certainty, the benefits of a reasonable offer. Then there are those who are not content to fold unless the adversary's blood is on the floor. Here again the Precautionary Principle comes into play. Will the rejection of the "best and last offer" end the negotiation and lead to a disastrous trial that exposes weaknesses in the case that have as yet not come to light? When to hold and when to fold.

There is also a time to open and a time to close. And this is the time to close. I opened with Ecclesiastes. I close with Shakespeare.

> *There is a tide in the affairs of men*
> *Which, taken at the flood, leads on to fortune;*
> *Omitted, all the voyage of their life*
> *Is bound in shallows and in miseries.*

Julius Caesar

I NEED A CONTINUANCE

The law practice brings me constantly into court for trials. When anyone refers to me as a Trial Lawyer, I lower my head and suggest by my expression that the description is misplaced. It would seem self-evident that those who are to be designated as Trial Lawyers must take pleasure in trying lawsuits. I confess that I do not. My pleasure is derived from continuing cases just before trial.

For years I was ashamed to seek help and guidance from others because I felt the vice was unique with me. I was recently released from my shame by a few remarks I ran across in a speech given years ago by Martin Littleton, one of the great advocates of the New York Bar in those days when forensic giants were in the land. He was the inspiration for Lloyd Paul Stryker, the author of *The Art of Advocacy*.

The remarks of Littleton to which I refer were spoken as he was addressing a course on trial practice conducted by the New

York Bar Association. Surprisingly, he stated that, although constantly engaged in trials, he invariably hoped for a continuance before every trial. He wanted the reprieve that the continuance would give so he could prepare his case just a little better.

I, too, always want a continuance. I want it whether I am appearing for the plaintiff or the defendant; whether the case be civil or criminal; whether my side of the case be good or bad.

As trial approaches, I yearn for sudden catastrophes and Acts of God that will claim precedence over such a triviality as a lawsuit. I conjure up a tremendous snowfall that blankets the courthouse under five feet of snow, paralyzing transportation and, of course, resulting in the continuance. I want power failures that close down all legal machinery. The closer to trial the continuance comes, the better I like it.

After reading Littleton's speech I spoke of my hidden vice to a friend who worked for years with one of Washington's finest. My friend said this leader of the bar would do anything for a continuance. Once in court he performed brilliantly, but it required a gun in the back to get him there.

Although my trial experience has not made me an expert trial lawyer, it has made me an expert at continuances. I can decipher my opponent's mind to determine the exact moment when he feels he needs a little more time to prepare his case. Sometimes he says that he is desperate to try the case, but on the other hand does not object to a continuance if I need one. Lawyers feel the need to purport to be anxious for a trial. They are like the Japanese sumo wrestlers who, before the match begins, make horrible faces and scream and hiss at each other with their eyes akimbo. I do not stand on ceremony. I suggest the continuance and close the conversation with a bit of harmless flattery concerning my opponent's reputation as an invincible, fearless trial lawyer who hates to be denied any opportunity to join issue.

If the definition of a Trial Lawyer is limited to those who are anxious to try cases, then there are few around who can qualify. There appears to be in all litigation a law which eliminates trial. It can be stated as follows: *A case that somehow can be continued will be continued, somehow.*

If that statement impresses itself upon you as an accurate abstraction of experience, then what are the implications?

First, litigation will remain in suspense unless there is an external force that inflexibly moves cases to trial and allows for no continuances. Any uncertainty about the trial date or the certainty of trial on that date will, according to the rule just announced, result in continuances rather than trials.

This brings us to an ancillary law, which I have not been able to formulate any better than this: *The first continuance is the most difficult to arrange, and all subsequent continuances become easier to arrange at the rate of numerical progression.* The first time a case is called the parties have made an acceptable preparation for trial and if compelled to go to trial they will either try the case or settle it. However, if the case is once continued, there is the suspicion that it will be continued again. The second time the case is called, the virginal certainty of trial has already been violated and a continuance is fairly acceptable. Almost any excuse will serve to continue a case the fifth or sixth time.

For instance, the first continuance will be allowed because of the severe illness of one of the parties. The second continuance will be allowed because of the illness of counsel. The third continuance will be allowed because of the illness of an important witness. The fourth continuance will be allowed because the file has been misplaced. The fifth continuance will be allowed because the depositions have been misplaced.

Once there has been a series of continuances, a psychological encrustment overtakes the case in the minds of the lawyers. They believe that they are dealing with one of those cases that will never be tried. There are such cases, you know.

It would be interesting to find the oldest case on the docket in any given jurisdiction and determine at what point the attorneys in the case made up their minds that this was litigation that would be continued *ad infinitum* and settled *sub silentio*.

INDECISION

Each trade or profession stamps its practitioner with a characteristic mark. There is a piece of thread on the tailor. There is the glazed eye of the accountant during tax season. The physician has become so accustomed to hero worship by his patients that he treats all about him as his rightful subjects. He is identified by that gentle bending of the body forward, which, in great men, must be supposed to be the effect of an habitual condescending attention to the applications of their inferiors.

What does the practice of law do to the lawyer? What does continued exposure to disputation do to his mind? Hazlitt's essay, "On Thought and Action," gives this case history:

Abraham Tucker relates of a friend of his, an old special pleader, that once coming out of his chambers in the Temple with him to take a walk, he hesitated at the bottom of the stairs which way to go—proposed different directions, to Charing Cross, to St. Paul—found some objection to them all, and at last turned back for want of a casting motive to incline the scale. Tucker gives this as an instance of professional indecision or of that temper of mind which having been long used to weigh the reasons for things with scrupulous exactness, could not come to any conclusion at all on the spur of the occasion, or without some grave distinction to justify its choice.

Hazlitt is describing a busy negligence lawyer I know who has grappled with the facts of so many automobile collisions that his own mind is an intersection of uncertainties, a crossroad of indecision.

The soldier is supposed to be a man of action. But he also can be reduced to indecision if, like the lawyer, he is poised between attack and retreat. General McClellan's indecision so provoked President Lincoln (a lawyer and hence an expert on indecision) that Lincoln wrote:

My dear McClellan:

If you do not want to use the army I should like to borrow it for a while.

Even the lawyer who donns the robe and picks up the gavel is not protected from indecision. Here is testimony given at a hearing before the Committee on the Judiciary of the United States Senate on February 15, 1966:

Judge Biggs: We had another case many years ago on which a judge also had developed what I think was a form of illness. He was unable to decide cases. ... He had a backlog of some one hundred and twenty-five undecided cases, and he could not decide them.

You can see by this excerpt that we are not dealing in trifles. But I would not have brought up the subject unless I could supply a cure for the war 'twixt will and will not. In fact there are several cures. I wish I could decide which is the best—or should I say the better. ...

MAY I SAY WHO'S CALLING?

Can you imagine practicing law without a telephone? No doubt it could be done. Abraham Lincoln did it. Daniel Webster did it. But once the telephone was invented, it became a necessity for the legal profession. Much of the practice of law takes place by telephone. Cases are settled. Court dates are assigned. Some lawyers spend their entire working day on the telephone.

When the phone was somewhat of a novelty, the early lawyer's directories had a special indication for those prosperous lawyers who would take long-distance calls collect. The passage of time is erasing even the remembrance of the old two-piece telephone with its forked handle for the receiver. It will soon be a feat of memory to recall yesteryear's telephone exchanges—names that were combined with digits to create a telephone number. The San Francisco exchange names including Yukon and Klondike brought to mind the great days of the Gold Rush. New York City had its

Regent and Chelsea. Washington, D.C., had its Adams, Capital, and Republic. The exchange names reflected the character of the city.

All of these have disappeared to be replaced by sterile, impersonal numbers and a telephone ritual that narrows and humiliates the caller. Numbers are dialed or pressed. The call goes through. The receptionist answers with the name of the law firm. The caller asks to speak to Mr. Holmes. The receptionist, in a slightly offensive tone, says, "May I say who's calling?" The call is then referred to Mr. Holmes's secretary. She too asks who is calling. The caller thus has identified himself twice without a hint as to whether Mr. Holmes is dead or alive, absent or present. All of this preliminary questioning (without a Miranda warning) suggests that a lawyer must carefully select the client or would-be client to whom he denies to speak. This reluctance to speak to those who call is unexplainable when coupled with the great desire of attorneys to find a clientele. It seems that lawyers wish to simultaneously suggest both availability and exclusivity. There is one lawyer I call whose secretary not only insists on having my name, she also must have the subject matter of the call. When she says, "May I tell him what this is about?", the devil within tempts me to say, "It's about his indictment." That would bring Mr. Unavailable to the phone.

In addition to the question, "May I tell him what this is about?" there is the further question, "And who are you with?" A friend of mine always answers that question with, "I am with my secretary. Who are you with?" If we continued exploring telephone ritual, we would all have some comment on the use of the hold button. People have spent a good part of their lives on "hold." Some of us seem to have the knack of always calling when the person we want is on the other line. We must then go on "hold."

It may be that you do not know how difficult it is for someone to reach you by telephone. The sure test would be to call
yourself while you are seated in your office with the door closed.
Dial your office number and then disguise your voice. It may be
that your receptionist and secretary will keep you from ever talking to yourself or, better yet, will put you on "hold."

THE DISCOVERERS

The Federal Rules of Civil Procedure commence with the civilized and entirely commendable statement that the just, speedy, and inexpensive determination of every action shall be the guiding principle of the rules. When the rules were presented to the bar in 1938, there was great rejoicing among those of goodwill. Justice would come with the elimination of surprise. Truth would prevail. Pretrial discovery—interrogatories, document production, and depositions—was a gift to the bar meant to complement the grand objective of Rule 1.

Time has shown that reality makes its own Rule 1. Simple interrogatories have become form interrogatories with subparts. The production of documents has become a satellite industry requiring paralegals with numbering machines, a coven of shredders, and Sherpas carrying bankers boxes. The mere deposition has become the killer deposition and the macho deposition. The passage from innocent idealism to the conduct of warfare by other means is part of daily practice.

Whenever I receive a set of form interrogatories with subparts, for example, I like to compare them with the ones in my collection. Most sets that now come my way are unimaginative copies of one of the six or more master sets minted in the 1950's during the era of the great interrogatory framers.

These pioneers had three objectives: (1) terrorize the deponent into dismissing the suit or settling under panic conditions, (2) request so much detail that it could never be assembled, and (3) obtain relevant information.

Although category one frequently has its desired effect, it sometimes does not: There are those who love to answer personal questions. The more there are, the better she likes it. I say "she" because the person I have in mind is a woman in her late fifties. She knows her social security number by heart and has prevailed twice in small claims court against the dry cleaner.

She is the woman who takes a seat in the front row of a shareholders' meeting and asks the chief executive officer whether he will submit his expense account for her inspection. She is the woman who has a congenital anomaly of the lower spine, one might say a spondylolisthesis, which renders her vulnerable to the trauma for which she seeks damages. She can recall each ache and pain caused or contributed to by the defendant's negligence.

A request to lift up her financial skirts causes her no apprehension. Not only is she undaunted by form interrogatories, she embraces the supplemental interrogatories, which dig yet deeper into long-closed accounts. She evades no question. She wishes to be forthcoming, and she likes to "state fully."

When her attorney receives the answers that she has carefully written out in longhand, he or she can look forward to hours of constant comment as the woman marches out fact, opinion, and surmise. She never fatigues. She has kept all receipts. She has calendars, diaries, and files bulging with letters, with each envelope attached. She is the one who has no reluctance to answer form question no. 26:

> Give the exact time when you first experienced pain, where you experienced it, was it temporary or permanent, how was it treated, has it ever hurt you there before, when, where, how much, how many, day or night ...

But there are still those who are not anxious to answer interrogatories. I have noticed recently this technique: "The interrogatory is objected to, and, without waiving the objection, the answer would be in substance, if an answer were given, that 'maybe yes.'" What does all that mean? Is it an answer? Well, maybe.

Another tool of discovery, as litigators are wont to say, is the document request. The ingenuity of counsel is on display chiefly in the definition of the word "document." The definition is set forth in the preamble to the document request. In the early, hopeful, trusting days, no preamble was needed to define the word "document." It was simply defined as "any writing." That definition no longer suffices. How is this for a preamble:

> The term "document" or "documents," as used in this Request for Production of Documents, means the original or a copy of the original and any nonidentical copy, regardless of original location, of any recorded, written, printed, typed, or other graphic material of any kind, variety, type, or character including, by way of

example but not limited to, the following: books; records; contracts; agreements; invoices; orders; bills; certificates; deeds; bills of sale; certificates of title; financing statements; instruments; expense accounts; cancelled checks; bank statements; bank books; receipts; disbursement journals; tax returns; financial statements; check stubs; promissory notes; resumes; address books; appointment books; telephone logs; worksheets; pictures; income statements; profit and loss statements; balance statements; deposit slips; credit card receipts; records or notations of telephone or personal conversations; conferences; intraoffice communications; postcards; letters; telex; partnership agreements; articles of incorporation; catalog price lists; sound, tape, and video records; memoranda (including written memoranda of telephone conversations, other conversations, discussions, agreements, acts, and activities) [if you have gotten this far, you are a real litigator]; minutes; manuals; diaries; calendars or desk pads; scrapbooks; notebooks; correspondence; bulletins; circulars; policies; forms; pamphlets; notices; statements; journals; postcards; letters; telegrams; reports; interoffice communications; photostats; microfilm; microfiche; maps; deposition transcripts; drawings; blueprints; photographs; negatives; and any other data, information, or statistics contained within any data storage modules, tapes, discs, or any other memory devices (including IBM or similar cards for information, data, and programs) or any other information retrievable on storage systems, including computer-generated reports and printouts.

Such a definition does not, of course, spring up overnight. It represents a Darwinian adaption to the need for survival. When the simple definition of "document"—a writing—was used, it was evaded. The lawyer who was able to evade became suspicious that others would be just as unscrupulous as he, so he made additions to the definition. Thus the coral reef grew. We know from military history that no matter how clever the offense, it is soon met with a more clever defense. The full meaning of the word "document" is still evolving. So is the meaning of the word "person," but that is a topic for another article, written perhaps by a lawyer-philosopher or attorney-clergyman.

Once received, a document request triggers action. The numbering machine is brought out and the dial turned back to 00001. It is inked up by a phalanx of paralegals who fall upon the documents with hourly-rate glee. After the numbering is completed, the chief of the litigation team steps forward. He must decide the big question: Should we do the copying in-house, or shall we send it out? When the copying is complete, the copies are lovingly placed in the document boxes with the hope that there are so many nobody will read them. As Sam Goldwyn said, "I read part of it all the way through."

Depositions are the most interesting discovery tools. I made the notes for this article during a deposition. Those in the room who looked in my direction must have assumed I was engrossed in taking notes of the testimony. Nothing of the kind. The questioning had long since passed the outer reefs of relevancy and sailed beyond the cape of materiality. I made the notes in order to combat deposition torpor.

A more common way to stay alert during depositions is to compare the lawyers' style of questioning. Recently I attended a deposition where the lawyer conducting the examination had decided to be nasty and abusive. He had great natural advantages. Each of his questions dripped with sarcasm. He was a good snarler. Each answer of the witness was met with incredulity.

The witness held up under this for several hours. Then the lawyer conducting the questioning sought to develop the utter absurdity of one of the answers given by the witness. As this continued, we saw that the witness had his own game. He had led the lawyer into believing that something was absurd when in fact it only appeared to be absurd to those who had no specialized background. Eventually, the witness wore down the lawyer, who fell back exhausted into the arms of sycophantic document pickers and summer associates. Napoleon in Russia came to mind.

There comes a time in every deposition when the clock strikes noon and thoughts of food become uppermost in everyone's mind. This gives rise to a discussion of whether the deposition should proceed right through the lunch hour or whether there should be a lunch break. Deposition macho requires an assertion that the march must go on, and there must be no lunch break. The first person who says he needs food reveals himself as weak and without the necessary stamina to be a great litigator.

Never accept coffee or fancy tea. Maintain an ascetic pose. Agree to stay as long as anyone wishes to stay. Never make a phone call. Give up the thought of the group ride at 5:30 p.m.

Go all night if necessary to complete the deposition. Never look at an airline schedule. Never have your two-suiter with you. Never admit you checked out of the hotel. Great litigators do not need food or sleep. When they do deign to submit a food order, they do it last, and they never order quiche or potato chips. They stick to tuna and "if you've got it, any diet soda."

One hears that the deposition procedure requires reforms. Lawyers have become too aggressive. Well, perhaps. But before we fall in with this criticism, let us take a look at the work of a lawyer who displayed warm zeal, maybe even hot zeal, in his deposition practice. The quotations that follow are from a case reported at 269 Ind. 630,383 N.E.2d 36. The opinion is part of this lawyer's post-deposition contempt case. It went against him. The lawyer is referred to as the respondent:

> We now find that the incident involved in this Count was the deposition of Henry Herschbach, an 82-year-old man. During such deposition, which lasted eleven days, the Respondent shouted at the witness, pointed his finger in the witness's face, and verbally abused the opposing counsel and the witness. The Respondent frequently accused opposing counsel of corruption, "hanky-panky," scheming to convert and steal funds and documents, falsification of records, swindling, suborning perjury; compounding a felony, dishonesty and evasive conduct. On the final day, during the course of the deposition and in the presence of the deponent, the deponent's wife, the plaintiff, and others, the Respondent told opposing counsel, John P. McQuillan, on three occasions, that Respondent was going to stick or put McQuillan's head in a "toilet bowl." During the course of the said deposition the Respondent also accused the deponent of dishonesty, lying, corruption, conversion, embezzlement, and other crimes. A number of these accusations were accompanied by Respondent pointing at the eighty-two-year-old witness, shaking his hands and fingers at the witness, and shouting at the witness.

★ ★ ★

This Court has examined all matters presented herein and now finds that during the course of the taking of Mr. Edward Schaeffer's deposition in 1970, the Respondent called opposing counsel, McHie, on the record dense, a culprit, so lacking in mental capacity as not being able to find his way to the toilet, too big for his britches, a skunk, a jack-leg, lazy, tricky, unfit to practice law, and a little yellow son-of-a-bitch. Respondent apologized to McHie on the next day. In November 1974, Respondent wrote McHie and amended his remarks to substitute "ring-tail" for "little yellow."

Such conduct may be unusual even in New York, or would it be? I recently saw a 75-page New York City transcript in which the deponent's only words were his name. The rest of the transcript was lawyer bickering ending in mutual Rule 11 threats, requests for costs, and accusations that courtesy yellow pads were stolen.

Trial practice for most lawyers is deposition practice. There we find the eloquence that was once on display in the courtroom. All that resourcefulness and skill in presentation must find an out-let in the speaking objection. This is the objection in which the lawyer tips off his witness about what is expected of the deponent if the case is to withstand a motion for summary judgment. There are efforts of late to ban the speaking objection, but it is the spit-ball of deposition practice. If the speaking objection disappears, something will take its place.

Such a replacement may come from the further development of the sanctimonious deposition preamble. In that technique, the lawyer tells the witness that the deposition is a desire to get at the truth. It goes this way in the eastern version:

Sir. I represent the defendant. I am going to ask you questions. My only purpose is to get the facts. If for any reason you do not understand a question, please ask me to restate it. If you need to take a break, just let me know. There will be no trick questions. All we want is the truth. That is what we are here for.

At a recent deposition, this preamble was given to the deponent, and, about 10 minutes into the deposition, the lawyer asking the questions put on his most sincere expression and sent forth a real trick question.

Here is what happened next. Counsel for the witness quietly told his client to leave the room. He then turned to Sanctimonious Sam and said, "You know when you recited all that baloney at the beginning of the deposition, the only person in this room who believed you was my client. He is a believing fellow. He is childlike. You just asked him a question that contains as already proven some facts you can never prove. I am going to call my client back into the room, and if you don't apologize to him, we are going to leave."

There was no apology, but there were no more trick questions.

Most deposition transcripts do not contain any exchanges of that quality. How would you like to pay out of your own pocket $1.50 a page for this, suitably framed in wide margins:

Q: Shall we go off the record?
Mr. Pendergast: Why should we? I like to stay on the record.
Mr. Reynolds: Yeah. Let's stay on the record unless somebody wants to go off the record.

Mr. Pendergast: Well, what is it?

Mr. Reynolds: Have it your way.

Mr. Pendergast: I will do whatever anyone wants. Is this off the record? I forgot.

Mr. Reynolds: No, this is on the record. Let's go off the record.

Despite such curiosities, we must not forget that deposition practice gives reasonably respectable work to the litigation camp followers: the court reporters, the litigation support systems, the software support systems, the accidentologists, the color-coded exhibit label manufacturers. And let us not forget the tab makers. What would we be without tabs? A Chicago law firm has three full-time tabbers. In one case I know of, the certificate of service contained four tabbed exhibits.

No one should let these details obscure the significance of what is happening. We are all participating in the second golden age of discovery. The memorable discoverers of the first were Columbus and Balboa. The memorable heroes of the second are not lonely figures on the oceans, but anonymous litigators sitting in conference rooms all across America. They press on, doing their best to resist eating too much of the host law firm's Danish pastry and striving earnestly to complete discovery—at least the first wave—before the cutoff date.

ABA Litigation Section

COLD CASH UP FRONT

When I ask law students what they would like to do when they graduate, most say that at some time in their career they would like to try a case in federal court. They will be disappointed. They are more likely to appear in federal court as a defendant rather than as a lawyer.

There is yet another disappointment in store for them. They will never get a cash fee up front. The client who pays cold cash up front demonstrates the sincerest form of flattery known to the legal profession.

These days, an associate in a law firm who brought in cash up front would be met with a series of pointed questions: Are you involving us in money-laundering statutes? Where did the client get the money? Why didn't he pay by certified check? Don't you know that the Criminal Code has 10 different reporting statutes concerning cash? The associate would be brought before a committee and grilled for three hours and then told to return the money and get a receipt and make a memorandum of the event and have the memorandum reviewed by a senior partner.

That was not always the case. Twenty-five years ago the criminal bar dearly loved to get cash in hand. The lawyer who got a good cash fee before noon walked with a spring to his step. He was open, friendly, optimistic, and generous. He lent money to his peers as needed. He invited those in his circle to lunch uptown. It may have been to Hammel's on 10th Street or to Harvey's on Connecticut Avenue, next to the Mayflower. Harvey's was special. The seafood was excellent. In addition, J. Edgar Hoover was on display at his own table, with his back to the wall.

Cash up front is entirely different from payment by check. The promised check may not be in the mail. Even if sent, it may bounce or be returned marked "Payment Stopped."

Robert I. Miller was a colorful member of the Fifth Street criminal bar in the good old days. He had a quick turnover, cash-up-front criminal practice. He carried around a big bankroll and did all his business in big bills.

In a proceeding before Judge David A. Pine in the United States District Court (I place the time in the 1950's), Mr. Miller cited a case during argument. The judge had reason to believe Mr. Miller never read the case.

Judge Pine: "Mr. Miller, do you have the case handy? If so, please hand the book up."

Miller, with a Toscanini-like gesture, handed the book up. He identified the page by placing a 100-dollar bill in the book as a marker. Judge Pine announced he was taking the matter under advisement. Judge Pine kept the book and the money for several months. He then had the clerk send the book back with a note attached to the 100-dollar bill. The note said, "Motion denied—order to follow."

Mr. Miller's career was interrupted when he was indicted and tried for first-degree murder. He shot and killed a leading psychiatrist who was having a love affair with Mr. Miller's wife. The jury acquitted Miller. He immediately returned to his all-cash practice with more clients than he could handle. There were giants in the land in those days.

The up-front cash fee that I recall most vividly involved an impressive-looking gentleman who wished me to do a few things that at the time struck me as clerical. In looking back I see that what he involved me in was not that at all.

The cash part went like this. I was asked what my fee would be. I gave a number, and then I was apprehensive that I had asked too much. The gentleman said that he would not only pay me the $300 fee, but he would add another $200 to demonstrate his faith in my competence. He put his hand in his pocket and drew out the wad. He removed the wide rubber band and counted out in 50-dollar bills the $500. I got more than I thought I should have received, plus a bonus. And all up front.

I asked if he wanted a receipt. He said, "Receipt? What for?" I should have known better. Big butter-and-egg men who deal in cash don't want to be bothered with receipts.

When he left the office, I put the money on my desk and counted it again. I pocketed the money and took a walk to calm down.

I walked from my office at Seventh and F streets to Pennsylvania Avenue and turned right. Within a few blocks I was in the Benjamin Franklin bookstore (long since gone), asking the price of the 1929 *Merriam Webster Unabridged, India Paper, New International*

Dictionary of the English Language With a Reference History of the World.
I had seen it in the window, and I hoped some day to buy it. Now
was the day. Cash is not to be thrown away on necessities.

The proprietor said it was in mint condition and rare. I
needed no sales talk. I knew all about it. I was there to buy—and
to pay cash. The price was announced, $35. I extracted a 50-dollar
bill from the roll. The book was taken from the window and
placed on the counter. It was mine. Although the book weighed
10 pounds, I walked out and resumed my stroll, with the
Unabridged under my arm.

I still have the dictionary. It defines "cash" as "ready money,
paid immediately." This won't do. The full flavor comes in the slang
definitions: cold cash, hard cash, spot cash, big bucks, bread, do-re-
mi, gravy, moolah, folding lettuce, mazuma, green bucks, and the
beautiful green.

If you had happened to walk past me as I strolled the avenue,
you would have heard me singing to myself:

As I walk along the Bois Boolong
With an independent air,
You can hear the girls declare
"He must be a millionaire."
You can hear them sigh and wish to die,
You can see them wink the other eye
At the man who broke the bank at Monte Carlo.

JUDGES

THE COURTHOUSE

This is that theater the muse loves best.
All dramas ever dreamed are acted here.
The roles are done in earnest, none in jest.
Hero and dupe and villain all appear.

Here falsehood skulks behind an honest mask.
And witless truth lets fall a saving word,
As the blind goddess tends her patient task
And in the hush the shears of fate are heard.

Here the slow-shod avengers keep their date;
Here innocence uncoils her snow-white bloom;
From here the untrapped swindle walks elate,
And stolid murder goes to meet his doom.

O stage more stark than ever Shakespeare knew.
What Peacock playhouse will contend with you?

Faded and yellowed with age, this poem, by Justice Wendell Phillips Stafford, has had a place on my office wall for many years. How or when I came by it, I cannot recall. Until recently I knew nothing about its author. The other day an old bencher mentioned Stafford's name and it triggered some research.

Justice Stafford, I've learned, was a Vermonter born in 1861. He practiced law in Vermont and also served as a Vermont judge. In 1904 President Theodore Roosevelt called Stafford to Washington and appointed him to the Supreme Court of the District of Columbia. What long forgotten political intrigues must have brought this all about.

Stafford served some 27 years as a local trial judge. He threw his considerable energy behind prison reform and other worthwhile projects. In time he established an outstanding reputation as a judge. He resigned in 1931 midst great praise for his contribution to the court and to his adopted city. He died in 1953 at age 91.

Justice Stafford's court, although a federal district court, was the local court of general jurisdiction because of the District's odd legal status. Thus Stafford was the daily spectator where all dramas ever dreamed were acted. What did the lawyers who appeared before Stafford think of this man who wrote poetry about the courthouse?

I spoke with three lawyers who did appear in Stafford's court. George Monk and Ed Campbell recall Justice Stafford as a no-nonsense judge who ran a strict court. They recall a mustachioed man, of erect posture, dignified and reserved. Campbell reminded me that justices became judges when the Supreme Court of the District of Columbia became the United States District Court.

Godfrey Munter recalls the judge as a somewhat irascible man with little patience for lawyers who drifted from the point or who were on the wrong side of the case.

The justice's published writings can be found embalmed in time's aroma in the law division of the Library of Congress. These consist of several books of poetry, an equity textbook, and a book of collected speeches. The speeches contain some worthwhile reflections on law and lawyers. They reveal a fully educated man who gave considerable thought to the practice of law. The naturally gifted lawyer for him was the lawyer with the power to perceive the true relations of things, a commonsense quality. "And who will not admit that common sense is always a gift of nature? If you know of any college that can confer an honest degree in common sense, let me know—I want to send my boy there."

Several lines of thought about the practice in Justice Stafford's day reveal themselves in the poetry and the speeches. His cases involved people and the tricks of human nature rather than large corporate or governmental interests. The cases related to life's passions and compassion and to the vices in conflict with whatever is worthwhile in human nature.

The lawyers who appeared before Stafford were specialists in the unraveling of secret human motivations. They eschewed the assembling of documentary evidence, the taking of discovery depositions, and the filing of Rule 11 motions. These were lawyers whose ambition it was to score a victory in a murder case, as Abraham Lincoln did with the use of the almanac and the phases of the moon.

How would Stafford view the changes 60 years have brought to the practice of law? No doubt the increasingly impersonal nature of the practice would not be to his taste. A number of the changes were summarized by Thurman Arnold in his autobiography, *Fair Fights and Foul.* The practice of law, he wrote, was far more personal years ago. Big-firm law practice nowadays is an anonymous practice. The names of the senior partners do not appear in the firm name. The law offices resemble large corporate headquarters.

The chief asset of the large big-city firm is the appearance it gives of institutional power rather than the personal reputations of its individual lawyers. There is no indispensable man or woman that the client seeks. As a partner gets a more lucrative opportunity, the partner persuades a less important client that some other member of the firm is just as qualified—or even more qualified—than he or she is. The legal talents are fungible. Any partner is presumed to be just as good as any other.

Stafford's poem came to mind again as I read an advertisement for the Courtroom Television Network. The ad announces that real live TV trials are on the way, "whether it's the L.A. cops or John Gotti on trial, or whether the issue is toxic torts or surrogate motherhood. TV brings the courtroom drama right into the home."

Justice Stafford, I feel certain, would have been repelled by the Courtroom Television Network. Litigants, as he saw them, were caught in a web of tragedy that often left permanent scars. Serve up these hapless victims as TV entertainment? Never.

THE VISITING JUDGE

Several weeks ago, I traveled to attend a court hearing cross country, out where the West begins. Local counsel directed me to the courtroom and gave me some background on the judge who would hear my motion. Then I was on my own.

I identified myself to the clerk, who told me and the other lawyers gathered around that a visiting judge would be taking the calendar. The assigned judge was engaged in a carry-over case and was unavailable. I questioned one of the local lawyers about the personality of this visiting judge. No one had heard of him. The corridor gossip was he had been sent in from a northern district.

As the judge took the bench, he requested that the clerk, because of her superior familiarity with the local practice, call the cases in any order she determined most efficient for the lawyers. Following the judge's direction, she divided the cases into a morning and afternoon calendar. The judge then announced that the lawyers on the afternoon calendar were excused until 2 o'clock. I was on the excused list but I had no place to go so I decided to remain and observe the proceedings.

The calling of the first case brought forward a young lawyer whose nervousness inhibited his flow of language.

"I don't know," he said, "whether to discuss the law or concentrate on the facts."

The judge leaned back comfortably and ran his hand through a full head of gray hair and said, "Would you like to know what I think?"

"I certainly would, Your Honor."

"Well, I think you ought to do what makes you feel comfortable and in that way you will be more helpful to me."

The lawyer's nervousness vanished. His voice became melodious. He found eloquence and spoke without repetition.

In another case, the lawyer for the defendant was incorrigible about arguing a subsidiary issue after the judge announced his ruling. Without a word of warning, the judge suddenly walked off the bench. He returned 10 minutes later and said to the lawyer who was still standing at the lectern: "You have so many good points I could not understand why you wanted to keep on arguing that bad one. I felt a few minutes would be helpful to you. Was I right?" Of course he was.

After each presentation, the judge discovered an opportunity to offer credible flattery to the lawyers. Good manners and attention to the small details that concerned others were all done effortlessly and without too much pedal, as the musicians say. Our visiting judge had taken Lincoln's maxim—with malice toward none—as his working principle. What an effect it had on the proceedings. Even the losers (I was one) were impressed by the judge's demeanor.

When the calendar was completed, the judge thanked the court personnel for their help, wished everyone well and declared his great pleasure at being with us. He waved his hand towards the well of the court and then he vanished through a side door.

Since that day I have tried to find out more about the visiting judge. My efforts have led to nothing. Nobody seems to know where he came from or where our mysterious stranger went. I should have guessed he was too good to be true.

OUTRAGEOUS IN
NEW YORK

Some weeks ago I had a meeting in New York City that took me to Foley Square, where the courts are located. I had planned to take the shuttle back to Washington when the meeting was concluded. But it began to drizzle. It was Friday. Rainy weather on a Friday afternoon is not a good time for the shuttle. Long delays, lots of tension, and a general uncertainty concerning the takeoff and landing. The waiting area fills with anxious commuters using personal telephones to investigate other arrangements and cancel appointments.

Experience has taught me to arrange a backup plan when I am in New York on a Friday. The backup plan is a reserve seat on the three o'clock Metroliner. The train ride is pleasant, and when it is raining along the eastern corridor it is time to take a nap and then meditate on ultimate issues, such as how the traveler who commences from he knoweth not where only to arrive at a destination he knoweth not can ever be said to have lost his way in this life of ours.

So there I was with a few hours on my hands until train time. My first thought was to take a cab to the Strand Bookshop at 12th and Broadway. It advertises itself as the largest used book-store in the whole world. It may be. I know of none bigger. The Strand is not an easy place to leave once it draws you in. It requires an hour just to examine the books on the tables and then hours more to examine the shelves. Well, there was not enough time to do justice to the Strand.

What to do? I decided to walk in on one of the local trial courts. New York trial lawyers have an intuitive grasp of the adversary system. There is always something to learn from them.

So I found a courtroom and took a seat. The trial judge was conducting status hearings. As he called each case on the calendar, the lawyers walked forward. The judge asked what the case was all about, giving the clear impression that he was unfamiliar with the file. His procedure was to listen to a few facts and then annotate the facts with comments concerning law and procedure. He kept the lawyers off balance by citing cases he said were decisive on the points in issue. Most of the time the lawyers did not know the cases cited. The judge acknowledged the ignorance and suggested that the lawyers look into the law a little more carefully. They would be well advised to be better prepared the next time the case was called.

In one of the cases, the judge was told by the plaintiff's lawyer that he was there on a very serious case. It involved the unlawful termination of an employee. The lawyer then said, "Judge, the termination was not only unlawful—the notice of ter-mination was submitted to my client on the day his father died. Judge, what do you think of that?"

The judge replied, "Well, I wouldn't do anything like that, but what are the damages?"

"The damages are the intentional infliction of emotional harm."

The judge then said, "Sir, where are you?" The lawyer was taken by surprise. He did not answer. The judge said, "Sir, you are in New York City. Do you understand that?" Now the lawyer understood he was to be made the centerpiece of the judge's performance. The less said, the better.

The judge continued. "Sir, in order to make a case of intentional infliction of emotional harm, you must show that the conduct is outrageous measured by the community standard. Sir, you are in New York City. Outrageous conduct is everywhere. It might be the norm. Did you read the *New York Times* today? Now I want you to know that I can read lips. I have learned to be a lip reader as I sit up here and watch you lawyers whispering to each other. Right here in this courtroom I have watched lawyers whispering that *I* am outrageous. Sir, I want you to take a seat in this courtroom and listen to the balance of the calendar. I assure you we shall bear witness to the most outrageous claims and defenses imaginable. And if that is not enough, when you get back to your office I suggest you take a look at *Friehofer v. Hearst*." I made a note of the case.

The judge, exhausted by his own performance, announced a recess. I went outside and mixed with the lawyers. I asked whether what I saw was unusual. No, it was not unusual. This judge had his own way of moving his calendar. He knew by heart a large part of the New York statutes and case law. He saw weaknesses in the cases that the lawyers had not seen or chose to ignore. As he exposed these weaknesses, many of the cases would settle.

When I got back to the office, I pulled up on Lexis the case the judge cited. It says that the plaintiff, in a case alleging the intentional infliction of emotional harm, must show that the defendant engaged in extreme and outrageous conduct that so transcends the bounds of decency as to be regarded as atrocious and intolerable in any civilized society. When this standard is applied, few cases of intentional infliction of emotional harm survive a motion to dismiss. Lexis did turn up one case that survived and the conduct, even judged by a New York community standard, was atrocious. I cannot bring myself to repeat the facts. They are just too outrageous.

A MAN OF LETTERS

There are lives a biographer in search of a subject cannot resist. The best candidate the legal profession can offer up is Oliver Wendell Holmes, Jr. Within the past three years two new Holmes biographies have been added to the respectable number already resting on the library shelf. These two are Sheldon N. Novick's *Honorable Justice* and Lisa Baker's *The Justice from Beacon Hill.* Yet another biography is in preparation.

The Holmes revival also brings us *The Essential Holmes,* a collection of Holmes's writings edited by Richard A. Posner, whose introduction gives a convincing explanation of why Holmes continues to fascinate:

> Only after Holmes's death did it become widely known that he had conducted for upwards of half a century a voluminous, erudite, witty, zestful, and elegant correspondence with a diverse cast of pen pals. Several volumes of this correspondence have been

131

published; the vast bulk, however—amounting I am told to more than ten thousand letters—remains unpublished. The published letters reveal that Holmes was a voracious, indeed obsessive, reader, of extraordinarily eclectic tastes, in five languages; a loving collector of prints; an astute student of human nature—in short a versatile, cultivated intellectual. Only recently has a set of love letters seen the light of day, addressed to one of Holmes's English friends, Lady Castletown. Holmes may have been America's premier letter writer.

Judge Posner goes on to declare that Holmes's career as a judge, as impressive as it was, may have been overshadowed by Holmes's standing as a central figure in the American world of ideas. What was the personal philosophy of this man of ideas? The Holmes philosophy of life is scattered throughout his letters in an informal, engaging way. It is based in large part on the writings of Darwin, Malthus, and others—skeptical of man's claim of special importance in the great chain of being.

Another letter-writing skeptic whose career overlapped Holmes's was H. L. Mencken. When Holmes's dissents were published in book form in 1930, he became the subject of a Mencken essay. Mencken found him to be a paradox:

Let us think of him, further, as a soldier extraordinarily ruminative and articulate—in fact so ruminative and articulate as to be, in the military cast, almost miraculous as a soldier beset by occasional doubts, hesitations, flashes of humor, bursts of affability, moments of sneaking pity. Observe that I insert the wary word, "occasional"; it surely belongs there. On at least three days out of four, during his long years on the bench, the learned Justice remained the soldier—precise, but daunted, unimaginative, even harsh. But on the fourth day a strange amiability overcame him, and a strange impulse to play with heresy. And it was on that fourth day that he acquired his singular repute as a sage.

If Holmes's letters had been available to Mencken, he would have discovered a man very much to his liking, much more so than Mencken set forth in his essay. Mencken said the same things in his letters as Holmes was saying. For instance, this letter of Holmes to Harold Laski:

> Personally I do not prefer a world with a hundred million bores in it, to one with ten. The fewer the people who do not contribute beauty or thought the better to my fancy. I perfectly realize that the other fellers feel otherwise and very likely would prefer to get rid of me and all my kind.

Lawyers might ask what kind of a trial judge Holmes would have been. Although most of his experience was appellate, he did sit occasionally as a trial judge during his 20 years on the Massachusetts bench. My guess is Holmes was a judge who kept his cases moving. No continuances. He would be quietly amused at the contrivances of the witnesses and the delaying tactics of the lawyers. Occasionally he would say something wise, disclosing a penetrating insight into the motives of the litigants. As a sentencing judge, he might give the maximum, but a well drawn, concise application for reconsideration, unblemished by grammatical errors, would receive favorable treatment.

I judge by Holmes's letter to Frederick Pollock, dated April 15, 1887, that Holmes was somewhat suspicious of litigants who exercised the right to trial by jury:

> I was interrupted at this point and am finishing my letter at the Worcester Club of a morning before going down to court and charging the jury in a will case. I shall expound to them what the meaning of undue influence is (so far as I know myself) and if they don't sustain the will I probably shall set the verdict aside. The man who wants a jury has a bad case—as an old Australian Judge said to me last year. I think there is a growing disbelief in the jury as an instrument for the discovery of truth. The use of it is to let a little popular prejudice into the administration of law—(in violation of their oath).

Well, those old Worcester, Massachusetts, juries always were an unpredictable, independent lot, but they were known to have done justice in will contest cases despite a misleading undue-influence instruction.

PEOPLE

COMES THE REVOLUTION YOU'LL PAY THE TWO DOLLARS

President Ronald Reagan, in his January 7, 1986, press conference, was asked some penetrating questions about the budget and its relation to the need for tax increases. His response caught him up in a hopeless tangle of numbers. He disengaged from the entire subject by saying: "So, I'm like that fella in the story. I'm still yellin', 'pay the two dollars.'" The usual commentary that follows each presidential press conference analyzed the implications of every statement. The exegesis that appeared in the *Washington Post* on January 9, 1986, examined the pay-the-two-dollars comment, but it misstated the origin of the phrase. It erroneously ascribed it to Milton Berle and other well-known comedians. There was no mention of Willie Howard.

Willie Howard was, in fact, "that fella in the story" who kept yellin', "pay the two dollars." How regrettable that Willie Howard, who died in 1949, was not alive to hear himself quoted with approval by the President of the United States.

Willie Howard was born in Neustadt, Silesia, on April 13, 1886. Franz Kafka was born rather close by in Prague, Czechoslovakia, just three years earlier. As I will show later, not only were the two born close in time and place, but they were close in the world of ideas.

Shortly after Willie Howard's birth, he and his family settled in Harlem in New York City. When Master Willie was still in short pants, he discovered his fine singing voice. He turned away from school and wandered the streets of New York singing for pennies in the cap. Those people taken with his voice probably failed to notice the darting movement of the eyes, the tilt of the head, the hunch of the shoulders, and the odd look of world-weariness assumed by one so young. There was within him an almost incommunicable sense of humor that was seeking expression.

In the book *From Ragtime to Swingtime* (1939), Willie Howard's first professional singing contract is reproduced. It was signed when he was five years old. It obligated Master Willie to perform his singing for a period of one year at the direction of John Leffler, a theatrical manager. Leffler agreed to pay Willie five dollars a week. The contract had this unique provision: "It is also agreed that in the event of the sudden changing, or breaking of the voice of the said Willie Howard, this contract becomes null and void."

Willie Howard and John Leffler renewed the contract from year to year until Willie, at age 14, suffered a reversal in his career. John Leffler arranged with Harry Von Tilzer, a songwriter and publisher, for Willie to attend vaudeville performances at Proctor's Theatre in Harlem. Willie's job was to spring suddenly up from the balcony seat and somewhat spontaneously sing the chorus of the Von Tilzer song that the performer on stage had just sung.

Harry Von Tilzer's career is part of the early history of American popular music. His real name was Harry Gumm. He adopted the name Von Tilzer for its continental tone. He turned out to be a songwriting prodigy. Among his many hits were "A Bird in a Gilded Cage" and "Wait 'Till the Sun Shines Nellie." His younger brother, Albert Von Tilzer, wrote "Take Me Out to the Ball Game." One of Harry Von Tilzer's songs, "On a Sunday Afternoon," sold, in one day in a New York department store, ten thousand copies. Von Tilzer wrote both the words and the music of waltzes, ballads, and comic songs. Irving Berlin, another prodigy, not only got his start in Von Tilzer's office, but he also got Von Tilzer to publish one of his first songs. Von Tilzer published George Gershwin's very first song, called "When You Want 'Em, You Can't Get 'Em, When You Get 'Em, You Don't Want 'Em."

An event in Von Tilzer's office in the early 1900's is given as the source of the words "Tin Pan Alley." It was Von Tilzer's custom to weave strips of newspaper through the strings of his old upright piano. This produced a tinny, mandolin-like effect. Monroe H. Rosenfeld, a frequent visitor to Von Tilzer's office, was not only a composer but also a newspaper writer always in quest of material. He had just finished an article about the music business and was casting about for a title. Von Tilzer happened to sit down and strum a tune on the trick piano. "I have it. There's my name!" exclaimed Rosenfeld. "Your piano sounds exactly like a tin pan. I'll call the article, 'Tin Pan Alley'!"

One afternoon Flo Ziegfeld, then a young theatrical producer, saw Willie's performance of a Von Tilzer song. Ziegfeld's public persona at that time consisted of his posturing as a dandy and a gambler. Ziegfeld's mature style as the affluent impresario is unflatteringly described in Ring Lardner's short story "The Love

Nest." Ziegfeld's early credit standing rested entirely on the fact that he was Anna Held's husband. Anna Held was a wasp-waisted beauty who became an international sensation singing "I Just Can't Make My Eyes Behave." Ziegfeld "discovered" her in France. He knew that if he could get her into this country he would have a valuable theatrical property. In those days, diamonds represented the theatrical manager's financial statement. Ziegfeld re-pawned his jewelry and cabled fifteen hundred dollars to Miss Held. She was so flattered by the gesture that she came to New York and placed herself under Mr. Ziegfeld's exclusive management. He then contrived what at the time was a fabulous publicity stunt. He delivered to Miss Held's hotel suite each day huge milk cans. He circulated the story that Miss Held's astonishing beauty was preserved by constant milk baths.

Ziegfeld thought Willie Howard's balcony performance would make a nice addition to Miss Held's presentation. He hired Master Willie to perform in his usual spontaneous way during Miss Held's appearance at the National Theatre in Washington, D.C. At the first performance, Anna Held sang a chorus of a song called "Mollie Shannon." When Willie rose on cue, he experienced, in the words of his contract, a "sudden changing, or breaking of the voice." His contract with Leffler was by its own terms "null and void." Ziegfeld fired him on the spot. Ziegfeld said he had hired a boy soprano who was now a basso.

When Willie Howard returned to New York, he found friends who encouraged him to forget his days as a boy singer and explore other opportunities. He soon discovered that the sad, strange look, which had gone unnoticed when he sang, had a comic quality. It created instant sympathy. He formed a team with his older brother, Eugene, and they worked up a comedy vaudeville act.

Their success in vaudeville is certified by a clipping dated September 23, 1911, from the *New York Star.* Willie was then only 15. It stated:

> There are few offerings that are more popular with vaudeville audiences than the act of Eugene and Willie Howard. These two young men have scored a remarkable success wherever they have played. They possess fine singing voices and their comedy dialogue never fails to score heavily. This week the clever team is proving one of the notable hits of the fine bill at the Bushwick Theatre, Brooklyn. Howard and Howard have received many offers to go into musical comedy but for the present they intend to stick to the two a day houses.

The article was accompanied by a picture of Willie Howard in formal attire, wearing a white bow tie and sporting a watch chain dangling from his left coat lapel, very much in the style of the times.

By the year 1912 Willie and Eugene Howard were vaudeville headliners earning $450 a week. They had performed in all the famous vaudeville houses both here and in Europe. In the space of a few years, America performed its miracle for them. Immigrant waifs were transformed into stars.

Willie and Eugene Howard were now ready to try their luck in a Broadway revue. The Shuberts included them in Shubert's *Passing Show of 1912*, which opened on July 22. It ran 136 performances. The appearance in *The Passing Show* stabilized Willie Howard's fame as a star performer. Thereafter, until 1948, there was hardly a season without Willie Howard appearing in a Broadway show in which he received star billing and star money.

Fred Allen, who appeared in one of Willie Howard's shows, says in *Much Ado About Me* that Willie "was a fine comedian, an accomplished dramatic actor, an excellent singer, and a versatile mimic."

In his long Broadway career, Willie Howard mainly appeared in short comedy sketches. Included was the sketch that became known as "Pay the Two Dollars." He first performed it in George White's *Scandals of 1931*. The show was unforgettable both for the music and the performers. The music was by Lou Brown and Ray Henderson. Ray Bolger was the featured dancer. Rudy Vallee sang "Life Is Just a Bowl of Cherries." Willie Howard joined Rudy in the final chorus. The original idea for the sketch was given to Willie Howard by Finley Peter Dunne, Jr., the son of the humorous writer who originated the Mister Dooley stories. An experienced sketch writer, Billy K. Wells, wrote the dialogue along with Willie.

The sketch commences on a New York subway. Willie plays the sad, inoffensive city toiler whose instincts tell him that the safe life consists of hard work coupled with the good luck not to become known by the authorities. He is with a friend who is a lawyer. This lawyer's personality demands that he challenge authority. He is intransigent and anarchistic. An argument arises between the two. Willie, in an excess of emotion, spits on the floor. The subway conductor directs Willie's attention to the sign that declares that there is a two-dollar fine for spitting on the subway. Willie wishes to pay the two dollars and withdraw into anonymity. His lawyer friend sees this as an opportunity. He must not permit his client to submit to authority. It is a matter of principle. There follows an escalation of penalties as the lawyer explores each appellate level. At every step Willie Howard pleads, "Let's pay the two dollars." He knows, with the peasant's perception, that the enforcement of the law is always in the right hands. But the lawyer is obsessed with vindication.

When Willie is sentenced finally to death, the lawyer directs his unabated energies toward obtaining a governor's pardon. Here he is successful. As they return home on the subway, Willie denounces the lawyer for destroying his life. He becomes worked up again and inadvertently spits on the subway. Blackout and curtain.

Despair is a major theme of twentieth-century literature. It is Franz Kafka's major theme. Kafka's characters are so poisoned by the bureaucratic secretion that they believe any governmental horror is not only possible but likely. This includes standing trial for crimes that are never disclosed. Any questions the defendant may have are referred to remote functionaries whose existence is only suggested and whose authority is subordinate to other more remote functionaries. The lawyer in Willie Howard's sketch makes the same mistake that Kafka's characters make. He believes that more resolution of purpose or more ingenuity will penetrate the obstruction and free the defendant. It is the nightmare become real.

The handy symbol of all this is the ticket. It may be a traffic ticket, or it may be the ticket for spitting on a subway. A challenge requires entry into the bureaucratic process. It consumes time and money. It feeds on confusion and misunderstanding. It is dangerous. The alternative is to submit and "pay the two dollars."

Willie Howard's familiarity with urban vulnerability came to him naturally as a 1930's walker in the city of New York. Kafka learned urban vulnerability in a different school. He was a claims examiner for the Workers Accident Insurance Company for the Kingdom of Bohemia, Poric Strasse 7, Prague, Czechoslovakia. He worked there from 1908 until his retirement in 1922. Most of those who have studied minutely all aspects of Kafka's life have failed to appreciate the full effect that his work in an insurance company's claims department had on Kafka's view of life. Every claim file is the same. It contains papers held in place by a brass clip. The first document in the file identifies the injured employee, the claimant, and describes in summary form the accident that produced the injury.

Of course, there is conflict between the employer's view of the case and that of the injured employee. The conflicts appear in the description of the accident and in the nature of the injury. Witness affidavits support each adversary's allegation. Medical reports either corroborate or discredit the worker's claim of injury. The worker is never seen in person. He has been transformed by paper magic into a file number, and his future depends on his file.

It was Kafka's burden to evaluate thousands of such files where the employee's assertions must be weighed against those of the employer. The files were piled on the floor, on chairs, on desks, and on windowsills, all tied with a red ribbon. There was never enough information in any of Kafka's files. Kafka, in order to do justice to both the employer and the employee, always needed more information. More medical reports and more witness statements might provide the decisive bit of evidence.

Kafka saw the process as both the insider and the outsider. He was consumed with guilt because he knew that until he made a decision, the injured employee was without funds. Every day's mail brought packets of letters importuning him for the decisive action he was incapable of taking. Kafka's letters to Felice demonstrate his inability to decide anything if there were competing points of view. Kafka was himself the faceless clerk that he saw as symbolic of the process which was without compassion and which demanded its tithe. Alan Bennett, in his play *The Insurance Man*, seeks to show that Kafka's *The Trial* was inspired by his work with the insurance company. In the play, life is portrayed as a process of repetitive injury and injustice.

Willie and Eugene Howard followed up their success with "Pay the Two Dollars" the very next year with another Broadway revue, *Ballyhoo of 1932*. It was in *Ballyhoo* that Willie Howard repeated his confrontation with the Zeitgeist. In a short sketch that opened with his appearance on a soapbox near Columbus Circle in New York City, he is a 1930's radical calling for fellow workers to join him in the attack on the injustices of capitalism. He exhorts each passerby to "rewolt." Only one specimen of the rabble pauses to be roused.

From time to time as the sketch was redone, the lonely member of the rabble was Al Kelly, *né* Kalisch, one of Willie Howard's great discoveries. Kelly was gifted in the art of intentional double-talk. He said very important things, controversial things, with emphasis, emotion, and gesture, but what was it that he said? He loved to tell how he once posed as a doctor at a medical meeting. He announced to his audience that he had been "able to rehabilitate patients by daily injections of triprobe and framis into the right differnarium which tranclucentizes the stolane producing a black greal which enables you to stame the clob." Notice the use of the word *framis*. Al Kelly used it so frequently that the word itself came to mean double-talk. John Ciardi, in *A Browser's Dictionary*, said that the word (or rather the non-word) *framis* appeared frequently in comic routines and then "as Pinocchio turned into a real boy, *framis* turned into a real word by biting off its own comic nose and becoming a label for what it once was."

As the sketch unfolds, Willie Howard declares that it is the capitalists who have silks and satins. It is the capitalists who eat strawberries and cream, extra-heavy cream. At this point, Al Kelly becomes enraged and declares, with raised fist, "But I don't like strawberries and cream." Willie Howard replies: "So you don't like strawberries and cream? A little too sweet for you, was it? Well, comes the revolution, you muzzler, you'll eat strawberries and cream."

Now, a few interesting coincidences. Al Kelly strongly resembled, in appearance and aggressiveness, Arthur Koestler. He was short like Koestler. He had a full head of steely gray hair low on the forehead like Koestler. He had the skeptical expression of Koestler. The "Comes the revolution..." sketch first appeared the same year Koestler gained admittance to the Communist party in Berlin, Germany—1932.

Koestler commenced his intellectual journey as a true believer that the common man, oppressed as he is by forces over which he has no control—the Kafkaesque—must "rewolt" against the oppressor and join hands with fellow sufferers. No doubt Koestler repeated many times in the several languages he spoke "Comes the revolution ... " This joining of hands as the first step in the march toward Utopia was given the name Dawnism by Hugh Kingsmill. At dawn, men of goodwill shall join together. By noon, they are fighting about principle. By evening, the majority, those in brief authority, find they can stifle dissent only through force. Tyranny replaces tyranny. Kingsmill submitted this view:

> Most of the avoidable suffering in life springs from our
> attempts to escape the unavoidable suffering inherent in
> the fragmentary nature of our present existence. We
> expect immortal satisfactions from mortal conditions,
> and lasting and perfect happiness in the midst of uni-
> versal change. To encourage this expectation, to per-

suade mankind that the ideal is realisable in this world, after a few preliminary changes in external conditions, is the distinguishing mark of all charlatans, whether in thought or action. In the middle of the eighteenth century Johnson wrote: "We will not endeavor to fix the destiny of kingdoms: it is our business to consider what beings like us may perform." A little later Rousseau wrote: "Man is born free, and is everywhere in chains." Johnson's sober truth kindled no one, Rousseau's seductive lie founded the secular religion which in various forms has dominated Europe since Rousseau's death.

Arthur Koestler's life tracked Dawnism. Communism for him was the alternative to Fascism. It offered a quick corrective to human nature's defects through politics. His experience in the Spanish Civil War taught him that Communism, as other forms of zealotry, survives only through despotism. He turned on his god that failed with the same energy he had devoted to his evangelism of the opiate of the materialists.

Koestler, once free of the dialectic, wrote with great insight on many difficult subjects. He was strangely attracted to the subject of humor—strangely, because he was quite humorless.

Koestler wrote the article on humor for the *Encyclopaedia Brittanica*. It is unfortunate that Koestler did not consult with Willie Howard beforehand. Things would have come off much better if he had. As it is, Koestler's comment on humor has its own unconscious humor. It reads like Al Kelly was the ghost in the machine that stated:

> The sudden clash between these two mutually exclusive codes of rules—or associative context, or cognative

holons—produces the comic effect. It compels us to perceive the situation in two self-consistent but incompatible frames of reference at the same time; it makes us function simultaneously on two different wave-lengths. While this unusual condition lasts, the event is not, as is normally the case, associated with a single frame of reference, but bisociated with two.

The only thing missing is a framis or two.

Koestler returned to an academic examination of humor in his book *Act of Creation*. He fails to solve the mystery of humor, as Freud fails, as Max Eastman fails, and as Bergson fails. All fail because the analysis of humor is as different from humor as lightning is from a lightning bug. The authors supply no answer to two key questions: If the author knows so much about humor, why isn't he funny at will, and why is it that people who repeatedly coin those funny one-liners know nothing of the science of humor?

By 1935, Willie Howard's truly creative period was over. By then he had an inventory of sketches he could draw upon as he needed. He required no new material. His audience would rather see him act out the old familiar routines than be surprised by something new. His working life consisted of arriving at the theater at seven o'clock in the evening and performing his 15-minute sketch in the first act of the revue and his ten-minute sketch in the second act. His life continued in this pattern year after year until shortly before his death. Although he appeared in movies and was an occasional radio performer, he had no real wish for a wider celebrity.

A retrospective study of his comic technique reveals that it was based largely on satire combined with the sudden superb swoop into nonsense. His sketch "French Taught in a Hurry" illustrates this. He first appears as a pretentious French academic instructing in French by speaking English in a most elegant French accent. Nevertheless, there are unexpected lapses into Yiddish and belligerent declarations concerning the primary importance of the student's paying tuition right on time, and any delay will be met with the relentless pursuit of the debtor in the "true French tradition."

He used his satiric gifts in his impersonations of Al Jolson, George Jessel, and Eddie Cantor. He first established an entirely accurate imitation of the singing style of each. Then, through bathos, he ridiculed their sentimentality.

Willie Howard's habitually grave expression was well suited to the delivery of wisecracks. I last saw Willie Howard perform in a revue called *Priorities of 1942*. In that show, he ended a short colloquy with a characteristic wisecrack. He was on stage with a singer who called herself simply The Incomparable Hildegard. Willie Howard turned to her and said, in his abrupt manner, "Hildegard, what is it that you do?"

She replied, "When I was eighteen years old my father gave me twenty thousand dollars to go to Europe and study voice with the best teachers."

"Well, that's quite something, isn't it? We'd all like to hear you sing."

With that, the pit orchestra started up, and The Incomparable Hildegard sang. When she had completed her elaborate performance, Willie jabbed her in the ribs with his elbow and whispered in a conspiratorial tone, "Honey, what did you do with all that money?"

The dictionary definition conveys little about the word *wisecrack*, defining it as a jocular smart remark, a jest. We need a broader definition to convey all that flashes off a good wisecrack. It sparkles with cynical city wisdom. The wisecrack is the perfect medium for expression of New York City's values. The city worships success, and Willie Howard had achieved success in the only terms his constituency understood. He had money, fame, and the ability to disparage by wisecrack any alternative value system. Another wisecracker, Damon Runyon, summed up the matter when he said that the fight is not always to the strong nor the race to the swift, but that is the way to bet them. New Yorkers are Darwinians.

The attempt to describe how and why an entertainer is funny must fail. It does no good to declaim about the genius of Chaplin, Keaton, Fields, and others. Their films are there to see, but their tricks are twice-told tales and a statute of limitations runs against them. The comedian's humor ages rapidly. Yesterday's comic routines are no longer consistently humorous. They are much like old family photographs. Time renders them naive. Fashions change.

The only humor that defies time is found in literature, where humor assists in understanding the utter strangeness and the unpredictability of human existence. An example is Gogol's short story "The Overcoat." It contains no jokes. It does contain the unforgettable character, Akaky Akakievitch. He is the long-suffering petty clerk, abused by all, who has sweet revenge when he returns after death to avenge the theft of his overcoat by stealing the overcoats of his tormentors. It is a story that does not go out of style. Willie Howard, at his best, conveyed the message and appeal of the Akakievitch spirit.

Murray Schumach, of the *New York Times*, wrote an extended article about Willie Howard that appeared on May 2, 1948. It was entitled "Willie Howard—the World's His Straight Man." Here is Mr. Schumach's description of Willie Howard a year before his death: "Away from the footlights Willie is morose in the grand manner of a punished deity—or maybe a small boy. Lines of woodcut intensity border his long upper lip, furrow his forehead and pinch the skin around his melancholy eyes. People seeing him under these circumstances feel sorry for him." It is the face of Akaky Akakievitch. Schumach says that behind the tragic facade Willie Howard was plotting farcical episodes to spring on friends and audiences—a Pagliacci in reverse.

Willie Howard lived to see his two epigrammatic reflections on the human condition become popular catchphrases. "Pay the two dollars" and "Comes the revolution ... " were as useful as subway tokens to a cynical New Yorker during the 1930's, 1940's, and 1950's. Strange that Bartlett preserved neither in the protective amber of his anthology of quotations. Despite this, they remain alive. "Pay the two dollars" found its way into the dialogue of the 1959 Hitchcock movie *North by Northwest*. The Cary Grant character, charged with drunk driving and other crimes, professes innocence. His mother, played by Jessie Royce Landis, disgusted over it all, advises, "Pay the two dollars." Of course the cream of the jest was when "Pay the two dollars" suddenly injected itself into the presidential press conference. It is just too useful a concept to disappear entirely. It continues to intrude at the most unexpected times and places, much like the ghost of Akaky Akakievitch as it grabs an overcoat off the back of an astonished senior office manager of a very important government bureau.

The American Scholar

SEÑOR WENCES

U*n bel di*, circa 1953, I was out for a stroll in New York City. My walk took me along Fifth Avenue, at the time the world's rialto. It was an avenue crowded with shoppers who were confident in the knowledge that anything money could buy was right there. Here was Tiffany's and there was Cartier's and Saks Fifth Avenue. As I walked along, my posture improved. I stepped with authority. I wanted to be accepted as an authentic member of the acquisitive elite. The overdose of materialism turned out to be homeopathic. I had the fugitive belief that I was about to perceive the substance behind this materialism, the continuity behind the transitory, and the laws that control who wins and who loses.

The general destination was Bartfield's Fine Bindings and Antiquarian bookstore on West 57th Street. In those days when in New York, I looked in on Bartfield's to check the stock. My walk took me past the Ed Sullivan Theatre, the home of the Sunday night television show. The billboard identified the next Sunday's performers. Among the names was Señor Wences, the juggler-ventriloquist. This brought to mind my own inept juggling efforts and William Hazlitt—William Hazlitt because of his essay on juggling and because of the tempting set of Hazlitt's collected works I saw at Bartfield's during my last visit.

As I entered Bartfield's I was afraid that Hazlitt might still be there. Could I resist again? With thoughts of Wences and Hazlitt and juggling spinning around in my head, I was a Bartfield's setup.

As I write, I see my set of Hazlitt's collected works in twenty-one volumes. It sits on its shelf, beautiful in its blue boards and black labels. Where will it go when I go? Perhaps back to Bartfield's. If it goes back to Bartfield's, it will be picked up by an interior decorator who doubles the price and places it in the library of a client who likes books in shades of blue.

Last August I took down Volume 8. It fell open of its own accord to page 77 and Hazlitt's essay "The Indian Jugglers." A reading of it explains why it was that the publisher, J. M. Dent and Sons, LTD (London and Toronto), had the courage in 1930, in the depths of the Depression, to print up sets of Hazlitt.

The Indian jugglers essay compares the uncertain success of intellectual attainment, such as writing essays and speaking in public, with the dramatic flair of astonishing excellence displayed by an Indian juggler keeping four balls in the air. Anyone can write an essay or make a speech and believe for the moment that what he did was pretty good. But can anyone try to juggle four balls, have them all fall to the ground, and still contend he is a pretty good juggler? With juggling and other such demonstrations of great skill, it is all or nothing. No in-between. It happens or it doesn't happen. Flattery, positive thinking, or meditation cannot disguise the failure.

Hazlitt opens his essay by saying that the Indian juggler tosses two balls into the air and catches them. This is what anyone can do. The essay continues with what the Indian juggler then proceeds to do. He keeps up

> ... four at the same time, which is what none of us could do to save our lives, nor if we were to take our whole lives to do it in. Is it then a trifling power we see at work, or is it not something next to miraculous? It is the utmost stretch of human ingenuity, which nothing but the bending the faculties of body and mind to it from the tenderest infancy with incessant, ever-anxious application up to manhood, can accomplish or make even a slight approach to.

Any miscalculation is fatal because

> ... the precision of the movements must be like a mathematical truth, their rapidity is like lightning. To catch four balls in succession in less than a second of time, and deliver them back so as to return with seeming consciousness to the hand again, to make them revolve round him at certain intervals, like the planets in their spheres, to make them chase one another like sparkles of fire, or shoot up like flowers or meteors, to throw them behind his back and twine them round his neck like ribbons or like serpents, to do what appears an impossibility, and to do it with all the ease, the grace, the carelessness imaginable.

This past August I saw television repeats of the *Ed Sullivan Show*. There is Señor Wences, in white tie, tails, and boutonniere, introduced by Ed Sullivan, whose awkwardness sets off so well the Señor's dandified elegance. There is the head-in-the-box character Pedro, the insolent puppet ruffian, unintimidated by Wences's decidedly aristocratic condescension. And there is innocent little Johnny speaking through Wences's gloved hand. Wences uses the catch phrases, "Deefeecult for you, eezee for me," and "'S okay, 's all right," phrases that caught on as popular expressions at the time.

What had happened to this distinguished, restrained, highly talented man? I decided to find out. I put in telephone calls to reliable sources. I was given the good news that Señor Wences was alive and well and living in New York City. I called his telephone number and spoke to his wife. She said Wences was in Spain on his annual summer fishing vacation. The tone of voice suggested that everyone knew Wences spent his summers fishing in Spain. He would return in October. She volunteered he was 99 years old.

When Wences returned to New York from his fishing trip, my wife and I met with him and his wife in their midtown Manhattan apartment. Each room of the apartment has on display pictures, playbills, and various awards corroborating Wences's incontestable skill as juggler and ventriloquist. The following framed poem is dedicated to Wences.

Let's give a hand to the Wences man,
   he made it talk to me.
With a flourish here, and an eyebrow there,
   oh, the things a hand could be.
When I was ten, you made me smile,
   with your head in the box routine,
And the way you threw your voice around
   was the best I've ever seen.

So here's a tip of the hat to you,
 and maybe a hand or two
For all the joy you've given us
 with your ventriloquist revue.

In the sitting room were two portraits in oil of Señor Wences posed as the middle-aged continental *boulevardier.* They were executed by a distinguished Spanish portrait artist, Lopez Mezquita, who has work on display at the Prado.

There was surprisingly little change in Señor Wences's features when one compares these portraits with the 99-year-old man sitting just below them. The facial lines were the same, the face of an El Greco or Goya Spanish *grandee:* the narrow face, the aquiline nose, the searching eyes. Wences said that those eyes required only a few seconds to size up the audience, to determine whether the audience was warm and receptive or uninterested and cold. When Wences toured with Danny Kaye, he would signal Danny backstage about what to expect by giving a good-news thumbs up or a bad-news one finger across the throat.

Wences was born in a little Spanish town, Penaranda, located near the university town of Salamanca. He was christened Wencesleo Moreno. Wences says that two hometown streets are named for him. Wences performed his ventriloquism in the movie *Mother Wore Tights* starring Betty Grable and Dan Dailey. When it plays in Penaranda, Wences gets top billing. Wences is the hometown boy who runs off with the circus to see the world and later returns to be welcomed back as a hero by those who knew him in his youth. Life accords such rewards only to the lucky few.

Wences's first ventures in ventriloquism were the calls he placed to one of his teachers. He imitated his father's voice and told the teacher young Wencesleo was sick and could not make it to school.

In his teens he signed on as an apprentice at the bullring. With some pride, Wences reported that he engaged in 300 bullfights. He described his style in the ring as "very quiet, very elegant." When he said this he paused and touched his left arm. He said he received a bad goring that required medical treatment. His doctor told him he must exercise the hand and arm in order to get a full recovery. This started him juggling. When his arm improved, he returned to the bullring.

In 1922, the Spanish Army drafted Wences and took him away for three years. When he went back to the bullring, he found that those he trained with had advanced in their careers and he was unable to regain his place on the ladder. He reluctantly gave up his real love, the bullfight, and joined the circus as a juggler.

My own interest in juggling commenced when I was 14 years old. I saw a vaudeville act at the Fox Theatre in Washington, D.C. The juggler was assisted by a beautiful girl who handed him the clubs and the hoops. I drew the obvious inference that juggling was a way to attract beautiful women. When I got home I commenced practicing. In time I learned the rudiments of ball and club juggling. I still have two clubs made by Harry Lind, the premier club maker of years ago. The Lind clubs are much heavier than the ones now in use. Lind gave a money-back guarantee: He would give a new club at no charge to anyone who complained of a loose handle on a Lind club.

Juggling, so Wences told me, required him to practice hours and hours each day. It might take him a year of practice to move from four balls to five balls. And that practice must be combined with real talent of a high order to enter the charmed circle of the truly accomplished. Anyone who wants to make a living by skill and wit must get an early start. Any delay and you will find you are a prisoner of the conventional. The parade will pass you by, and you will be in class studying for the college entrance exams. Wences entered that circle, and he has stayed in touch with the other star performers.

By the late 1930's Wences had compressed into a 19-minute performance the years of onstage trial and error, the hours of practice, and a discerning talent to amuse. He worked with Johnny, the little blond-haired boy who spoke through Wences's gloved left hand. To his right was Pedro, the head in the box. Pedro wants to get out of the box. Wences, as the ventriloquist, gives a voice to Pedro, a muffled voice in the box. As Wences slowly opens the box, Pedro's voice becomes clear. When Pedro gets out of line, Wences says to Pedro, "Back in the box," and Pedro's voice changes as the box closes. For no particular reason Pedro has eyeglasses and a moustache.

Wences told no jokes. The talking consisted of bizarre farcical patter delivered in an unusual, Spanish-accented, loud whisper. What was said sounded as if it should be understood, but just exactly what was said remained uncertain. Wences juggled the three distinct personalities—his own, Pedro's, and Johnny's. In this trialogue, each participant is wary of the other. All three suddenly grow assertive. And just as suddenly they convert to an exaggerated and pompous civility.

The act exerted a peculiar appeal. Imitators such as Chevy Chase and Robin Williams did Wences knock-offs. In the movie *The In-Laws*, a Banana Republic dictator does a Wences imitation. Pedro appeared in commercials. In Egypt, King Farouk took time out from his debauchery to arrange a Wences command performance.

The relationship between a ventriloquist and the ventriloquist's dummy is a self-induced schizophrenia. Who is who? Erich von Stroheim, in one of the first talking pictures, *The Great Gabbo*, played an egomaniacal ventriloquist whose better side appeared only as the ventriloquist's dummy, Mr. Otto. In the 1978 movie *Magic*, Anthony Hopkins plays the magician ventriloquist; his dummy takes control and manipulates his master into committing a series of murders. It would take a Robertson Davies and another *Deptford Trilogy* to explore the full Jungian possibilities of the theme.

Once Wences settled on that 19 minutes, he used it to earn a very good living for the rest of his long working life. There was no overhead. Wences talked to his own left hand and a head in a box. It was a ticket to the leading cities of the world. At one point Wences interrupted his travels for a seven-year stay in Paris. He paid his way by performing nineteen minutes, twice a day, at the Crazy Horse Saloon. What a treat for a dandy. Plenty of money, plenty of time, and the City of Light exposed to the contented *flâneur*.

As we talked Wences picked up three well-worn juggling balls. He said his arthritis made it very deefeecult to do any more juggling. I took the balls and did some juggling for the master. He was mildly amused at my presumption.

In the 1940's Wences was performing in San Francisco. His wife-to-be, Natalia, appeared on the bill as a dancer. They say they disliked each other when they first met. A year later they met again in New York. They decided they should make a life together. Natalia was born in Russia. She and her parents left Russia when Natalia was young, and they took up residence in Berlin, where Natalia studied ballet. When the Nazis took over in the 1930's, she went to Paris and joined the Corps de Ballet of the Follies-Bergère. She came to the United States with a dance troupe in 1934. Natalia is fluent in seven languages. She speaks English with a British accent. She and Wences prefer Spanish as their first language. Her bookcase has an eclectic selection of books in Russian, Spanish, French, and English.

Wences's career intersected with the Television Age. He became a regular on Ed Sullivan's Sunday night show where he appeared some forty-eight times. Wences began at the rate of six hundred dollars a performance for 12 minutes. As his popularity increased, he demanded and got seven thousand dollars a performance for that same 12 minutes.

Wences's career and Edgar Bergen's overlapped. Bergen's success with Charlie McCarthy brought Bergen generous contracts in radio and in the movies. Although Wences never achieved the popularity with the public that Bergen did, it was Wences whom the professional ventriloquists regarded as the more skillful of the two.

Wences recalled that when Edgar Bergen appeared at the London Palladium a few weeks after Wences, Bergen was not well received. Bergen's ventriloquism had none of the Wences virtuosity. Wences pushed the art of ventriloquism to extremes—he could smoke a cigarette, turning out smoke rings, all undisturbed by the spirited dialogue he was carrying on with Pedro. Wences's way of smoking his *Galois* was slow and dramatic, as Don José smoked his cigarette when he met Carmen at the cigarette factory.

Wences received his bookings through the William Morris Agency. Edgar Bergen received his through Music Corporation of America. MCA offered Wences substantial money to switch to MCA. Wences was suspicious of the offer. His suspicions proved to be well founded. He learned that Edgar Bergen would have used his influence with MCA to keep Wences away from any appearances that would reflect unfavorably on Edgar Bergen. Wences stayed with William Morris.

Bergen was aware that his success did not rest on his skill as a true ventriloquist. He relied on the best gag writers available. At the height of his popularity, he was a radio personality. Bergen had a comedian's sense of timing that was the envy of other comedians. Jack Benny, after appearing on Edgar Bergen's radio show, said he got so confused waiting for Bergen and Charlie McCarthy to stop throwing dialogue around that when he finally got to a joke of his own, he read it like a question.

The competition between Edgar Bergen and Señor Wences ended quite dramatically. In 1978 Bergen announced his retirement and performed for the last time on September 29th at Caesar's Palace in Las Vegas. When he finished his performance, Charlie said goodbye to the audience and to Bergen. Then Bergen said, "All acts have a beginning and an end, and I think that time has come for me. So, I think I'll just pack up my jokes and my friends and, as the days dwindle down to a precious few ... September ... November ... " That night John Edgar Bergen, age 75, died in his sleep.

This past December, my wife and I attended the New York Friars Club dinner honoring Señor Wences. The guests included a number of Wences's old theatrical friends. They exchanged their thrice-told tales of days gone by. The cream of these jests was told by Tony Belmont, a musician and theatrical promoter. He held the floor with this story.

When he was a young boy of 10 or 12, Belmont was a pretty good jazz drummer. He wanted to meet some of the headline jazz performers. An older friend suggested to Belmont that he could slip him past the doorman at the Metropole at 50th and Broadway, where the jazz musicians performed. Belmont would be disguised as a midget. They went to the Metropole. They got past the doorman. Once inside Belmont is introduced to Dizzy Gillespie as a midget drummer. Gillespie asks Belmont if he knows the drum breaks in "Caravan." Belmont says he does. Dizzy points to the drums. Belmont takes his position. Everything goes well. Belmont is giving a great performance. He becomes excited at the second big drum break. In one of his violent jumps to get added percussion on the skins, his back hits the spring doors behind him that open to the alley. The doors spring open. Belmont falls backward into the alley behind the Metropole. The doors spring shut. Belmont gets up, cleans himself up, and runs around to the front of the Metropole to get a report on his drum playing. The doorman stops him. No kids allowed.

A few days later Belmont catches up with his patron. What did Dizzy think of me as a drummer? What did he think! Dizzy said you are the greatest midget drum magic escape act he ever saw. Can the stunt be repeated? If so, bookings in Las Vegas await.

Wences arrived at the Friars Club at six that evening. The dinner party did not break up until close to eleven. Wences showed no signs of fatigue. He was treated with great respect by all in attendance. He appeared observant of whatever went on about him, but not engaged with it—a little aloof. Stories were told about him, but he told none about himself. He maintained the reticent pride of one who had found a way to use his stage tricks to play the picaro's trick on life itself. "Deefeecult for you. Eezee for me."

George Santayana had someone such as his fellow country-man, the elegant Señor, in mind when he noted in *Reason in Art* that the artist constructs a world of his own: "... nor is he concerned with the chance complexion of affairs in the actual world, because he is making the world over, not merely considering how it grew or how it will consent to grow in future."

Hazlitt concludes "The Indian Jugglers" essay with a tribute to John Cavanagh, a highly skilled handball player who, like the Indian juggler, did his one thing better than anyone else. Hazlitt describes Cavanagh as a player who was not "ineffectual—lumbering like Mr. Wordsworth's epic poetry, nor wavering like Mr. Coleridge's lyric prose, nor short of the mark like Mr. Brougham's speeches, nor wide of it like Mr. Canning's wit, nor foul like the *Quarterly*, nor *let* balls like the *Edinburgh Review*."

I was present on April 20, 1996, to discuss all these matters with Natalia and the Señor at his hundredth birthday. As his friends looked on, Wences stalked, *capa y espada*, the elderly gentleman with the scythe. The Señor promptly dispatched his adversary, removed and tossed his white gloves to the table. In Pedro's voice he announced that he was departing for Spain to take up his annual five-month fishing vacation and he would see us again in the fall.

The American Scholar

CURTAIN UP

We all know what the big time is. It's the tops. It's Cole Porter. It's the Colosseum. There was a time when big time conveyed a special meaning, its vaudeville meaning. It was twice a day, and both performances in the best vaudeville houses. The small time was five times a day in shabby theaters.

Some 10,000 vaudeville performers, gypsies with luggage, were working or looking for work in the years from 1920 to 1930. It was a work force made up of song and dance men, deadpan comics, magicians, animal acts, acrobats, iron jaw acts, good actors, bad actors, jugglers, knockabouts, and musicians. Everyone's goal, including the animals', was the big time. Gilbert Seldes writing in 1924 described what was required to make the big time:

> They have to do whatever they do swiftly, neatly, without lost motion; they must touch and leap aside; they dare not hold an audience more than a few minutes, at

least not with the same stunt; they have to establish an immediate contact, set a current in motion, and exploit it to the last possible degree in the shortest space of time. They have to be always "in the picture," for though the vaudeville state seems to give them endless freedom and innumerable opportunities, it holds them to strict account; it permits no fumbling, and there are no reparable errors. The materials they use are trivial, yes; but the treatment must be accurate to a hair's breadth; the wine they serve is light, it must fill the goblet to the very brim, and not a drip must spill over. There is no great second act to redeem a false entrance; no grand climacteric to make up for even a moment's dullness.

The big time was controlled by a group of monopolists, impresarios, sporting astrakhan-collared overcoats with an upper left hand pocket carrying a brace of Havana cigars protecting the heart of stone. They selected the few whose names stood three feet high at vaudeville's palaces of pleasure.

The big time followed a careful ritual. It had eight acts. The show opens with the professor, the leader of the band, tapping his baton. The lights go dim and music is in the air. The opening act, acrobats or jugglers, knocks about as the audience takes its seats. In the deuce spot is a double act singing and dancing. The number three act is a sketch. The fourth spot, just before intermission, is filled by someone who thinks he should be the headliner. The real headliner is on next to closing. That's the place to be, next to closing, the third act after intermission. The final act, it is the acrobats again.

When vaudeville was king its performers were always live, very much alive. The words "in person" and "live" were unnecessary on the show bill. It was life jumping over the footlights into the audience. Each performance was now or never. This placed an urgent responsibility not only on the performer but on the audience as well. The great performances must be fixed in the memory to be recalled from time to time. And if the performer returned next year any inaccuracy in the memory could be corrected.

The same technology that gives us, at the flick of a switch, the performance we desire, removes the thrill and the mysterious pathos that comes with immediacy, with a performance that will never be seen just that way again and a performer whose name next week may appear in a black-bordered theatrical necrology, leaving only props and racks behind.

The theatrical neonatologists identify the 1900's as the birth of big time. The theatrical coroners identify 1932 as the death of big time, when the very top of the big time, the Palace Theatre, closed down two-a-day vaudeville, a victim of radio, movies, the Depression, and the heartless malefactors of great wealth.

Robert Taylor's biography of Fred Allen, a man who played the big time, tells us all the facts worth having about Fred Allen, his circle, and his times. The Taylor biography and Robert W. Snyder's book about New York vaudeville, the two taken together, give a *couleur-de-rose* tint to a back page of American history. They provide what may be the last good look at vaudeville's short life, some thirty years of clamor up the golden staircase to a tinseled paradise consisting of fame and the big money for the few who made it.

Vaudeville was real American-style opportunity. Put together a good fifteen-minute act and, if it catches on, you have a shot at the big time.

The act, if a hit, would last a lifetime. Didn't Smith and Dale and didn't Willie West and McGinty do the same act year in and year out, always big time and always working? Snyder describes the process:

> Despite the odds against success, vaudeville was egalitarian in a competitive way. Vaudeville was far more open than the formal professions: the key criterion for success was the ability to put an act over. The start-up costs were minimal. Performers invested their ability to sing, dance, tell a joke, or do somersaults in midair. Their capital was in their bodies and their craftsmanship. Family lineage or formal education meant little.

It worked just that way for Fred Allen. We learn from Taylor's biography that Fred Allen was born in the Cambridge, Massachusetts, area and christened John Florence Sullivan. His mother died when he was three. He had no memory of her. His father, a somewhat pathetic figure, with a weakness for alcohol, worked as a library bookbinder. Aunt Lizzie was Fred's father and mother. She struggled to keep her household together with the domestic versatility required of those with barely enough money to cover the necessities. Fred attended the Cambridge public schools. He later joked that he passed through Harvard on his way back and forth to Aunt Lizzie's.

Fred's father used all his Boston connections to connect Fred with the Boston Public Library as a runner. In his idle library time the fourteen-year-old Fred took up juggling. He commenced his challenge to the laws of gravity by crisscrossing three balls in the air. When he learned to do this seemingly impossible stunt he astonished himself by juggling clubs, and hats, and then doing his trick with the three cigar boxes. He transformed himself from a nobody to a somebody who could make an audience say "I wish I could do that."

Rather quickly he found opportunities to play the show-off. Amateur shows led to the vaudeville years. Taylor writes that Fred's footloose "vaudeville days of his youth remained the brightest in memory."

The name Fred Allen came into existence only after John Florence Sullivan used up four other stage names. Freddy James was his name when he toured the Australian vaudeville theaters. On his return to America he discarded Freddy James in favor of Fred Allen. He needed the new name to conceal the fact that he was playing in two New York vaudeville houses at the same time. Freddy James was a self-effacing performer billed as the World's Worst Juggler. Fred Allen was a well dressed, somewhat pushy swell, described on the show bill as A Young Fellow Trying to Get Along. Most performers used explanatory tags. Al Jolson was The World's Greatest Entertainer. Eva Tanguay was The I Don't Care Girl. Joe Jackson was The Funniest Cyclist in the World, Ted Lewis was The High Hat Tragedian of Jazz, Ed Wynn was The Perfect Fool.

Fred Allen did something Freddy James didn't do. Fred Allen not only juggled, he played the guitar, but not too well. He continued in the small time, running here and there experimenting with the jokes and the tricks. He perfected his walk-on and his encores. And then the unexpected call. E. F. Albee, of the Palace Theatre, needed a quick fill-in act. One of the unique by-products of New York City's experiment with the puritanical was an ordinance prohibiting acrobats from appearing in vaudeville theaters on the Sabbath. No other acts were prohibited. Mr. Albee had the four Boises, flying acrobats, opening the Palace Sunday matinee before he discovered it was against the law. Was Fred Allen available to open the program at the Palace? Allen played the matinee. He was cancelled before the evening performance. So the year

1918 marked his rise to the big time and then the tumble back into the small time. Between 1918 and 1922 Fred Allen was both a small timer and a big timer, but mostly a small timer. Gradually the juggling faded and the gifted satiric monologuist emerged.

In 1922, Fred Allen's career took off. He connected with a Broadway revue, *The Passing Show of 1922.* He helped write its comedy sketches. He found he not only could perform comedy, he was now a special-material man. *The Passing Show* brought another benefit. He met a chorus girl named Portland Hoffa. In time they married and lived happily ever after.

In 1926 an act he wrote got him another call to the Palace where he appeared with his partner, Bert Yorke, a vaudeville song and dance man. The act knocked 'em dead, stopped the show, brought the house down, scored a socko hit. They not only played the full week, they were held over. From there it was nothing but the big time for Fred. He made lateral moves into Broadway revues including *The Little Show* with Clifton Webb and Libby Holman, an odd trio if there ever was one. Clifton Webb later cast aside his dancing shoes and turned himself into a dandy of a movie star famous for playing Mr. Belvedere. Libby Holman made new headlines when she beat a murder rap after R. J. Reynolds's son, who was in love with her, was found dead.

Fred Allen also discovered that he could write. Taylor comments that by 1931 Fred Allen had developed his mature, comic prose style. The *New Yorker* published an article of his entitled "Don't Trust Midgets."

As the 1920's danced to an end many vaudevillians crossed over into radio and the movies. Those who controlled vaudeville were displaced by the money men who saw that the new forms of mass entertainment, the radio and movies, would replace vaudeville.

Joseph P. Kennedy contributed to the transformation. Marian Spitzer, in her book, *The Palace*, gives the details of a transaction that theatre people of the time enjoyed retelling. It was the story of one bully kicking another. Kennedy acquired control of a small motion picture company and built it into a successful operation. Through a series of maneuvers using the motion picture company as a cloak, Kennedy bought into the E. F. Albee interests that controlled The Palace, the same E. F. Albee who put Fred Allen into the big time. Albee was not well liked. He was cruel and over the years destroyed many lives. Kennedy gained control of the Albee interests before Albee knew what was happening. Albee treated Kennedy as a junior partner. Shortly thereafter Albee appeared at Joe Kennedy's office to talk business. Kennedy said: "Didn't you know, Ed? You're washed up. You're through." Albee's closest friends said it couldn't have happened to a more deserving fellow. When Albee died in 1930 an attendee at the final ceremony reported it in bottom line terms: "The funeral played to a small house."

When Fred Allen was first asked what he thought of radio he said "Not much. When I buy a piece of furniture I don't want it to talk to me." Despite that observation, in October 1932 he was on the air with the "Linit Bath Club Review," Sunday night at nine. The Linit show made Fred a celebrity. He later would declare that a celebrity is "a person who works hard all his life to become well known, then wears dark glasses to avoid being recognized."

Fred Allen took control of radio comedy in 1934 with an hour-long program sponsored by Ipana toothpaste and Sal Hepatica. First known as the "Hour of Smiles," it was retitled "Town Hall Tonight." It opened with Peter Van Steeden's Ipana troubadours playing "Smile, Darn Ya, Smile." It became a Wednesday night standard and remained so until 1942. Fred Allen tried to write

171

most of the program himself, but in time he found it impossible and he picked up "the boys," Arnold Auerbach and Herman Wouk. After the Wednesday evening broadcast the boys went to the Stage Delicatessen, whose proprietor Max Asnas was nicknamed by Fred as the Corned Beef Confucius. The boys put together the outlines of the next week's program. Fred went to bed early Thursday morning. When he got up he went to the neighborhood YMCA, boxed a few rounds, played handball, jogged, and tossed the medicine ball. Each Wednesday it started all over again.

In 1936, Taylor tells us, Allen's radio audience numbered some 20 million. He delighted his audience with things such as his feud with Jack Benny and the tours through Allen's Alley. In 1945 the Alley acquired the cast by which it is best remembered. Kenny Delmar was Senator Claghorn. Parker Fennelly was Titus Moody, the New England farmer. Peter Donald was Ajax Cassidy, the stage Irishman. Minerva Pious was Mrs. Nussbaum entangled in Yiddish-American idioms.

Every now and then Fred Allen brought back one of his vaudeville friends. These included Jack Haley, Doc Rockwell, and George Jessel. Fred Allen was in awe of Jessel's vulgarity, bathos, and mythomania. In one sketch Allen said he was constructing a vaudeville monster and he wished permission to use Jessel's voice. Jessel accommodated. When Allen reminisced about vaudeville he told stories about the closed world of the performer and the need for self-promotion. He spoke of a comedian named Bert Frohman. One time Frohman opened in Baltimore to an empty house. There were only six people in the audience. When Bert met his friends later, he said "Baltimore was terrible—only seven people in the audience."

In 1948 ABC positioned the program "Stop the Music" against Fred Allen's time. Anyone who wants to be reminded of "Stop the Music" can rent Woody Allen's *Radio Days* from the video shop. The movie opens with a scene showing second-rate burglars engaged in their work in a lower-middle-class household in old New York. "Stop the Music" is on the radio. The phone rings. One of the burglars picks up the phone. Bert Parks is on the line. He wants to know the name of the song. The burglar guesses it. Three days later the tragedy of the burglary is nullified when the innocent victims are deluged with the prizes—refrigerators, vacuum cleaners, and a motorcycle. Fred Allen would have loved the scene, but it was "Stop the Music" that stopped Fred Allen. His ratings dropped and he was dropped.

Although Fred was unaware of it for a while, his career as an entertainer was over. He also found that his health was not good. In 1949 he suffered a minor stroke. He recovered and he made appearances from time to time on radio. He especially enjoyed mixing it up with the smart alecs on "Information Please." He tried television but it didn't work. Neither did his movie appearances. His time had passed.

He turned to writing. His first book was *Treadmill to Oblivion*, a story of radio's decline and fall. The book was well received. He started another, an autobiography. Before Allen died, suddenly, of a heart attack on March 17, 1956, he had completed his recollections. The book was published shortly after his death and entitled *Much Ado About Me*. It is not the extended press release coupled with a yearning for the roar of the greasepaint and the smell of the crowd that one finds in most theatrical autobiographies. It contains mature observations on long-ago Boston and the vaudeville life, its ups and downs.

Fred Allen comes through as a man of quality. The early habits of trying to improve his act lasted a lifetime. In contrast to most theater people he was introspective, frugal, and intelligently generous. During his travels he got into the habit of buying hick-town real estate. I once talked to a lawyer who knew something about the ultimate value of those properties. They were sold at high prices when Portland Hoffa died some years after Fred. Fred had a very good eye for a real estate bargain.

Mr. Snyder, in his book on New York vaudeville, refers to Fred Allen's *Much Ado About Me*. Snyder has done all the other required reading: Gilbert Douglas's *American Vaudeville*, Joe Laurie's *Vaudeville: From the Honkey-Tonks to the Palace*, the Samuels' *Once Upon a Stage*, Bill Smith's *Vaudevillians*, and many more such books. He also went into the field and interviewed the big- and the small-timers still among us.

I hope Snyder, during his research, caught the show-off bug and taught himself to juggle while playing "Bye Bye Blues" on the twin kazoos. If he did, we will turn him over to Benjamin Franklin Keith, Albee's partner. A kickback arrangement will get him the next-to-closing spot at the *New Old New Palace,* way up there in the big blue sky. The curtain's going up. Mr. Leader Man, something in ragtime, if you please ...

The American Scholar

WORDS AND MUSIC

... there is a certain number of artists who have a distinct faculty of
their own by which they convey to us a peculiar quality of pleasure
which we cannot get elsewhere; and these, too, have their place in
general culture.

Walter Pater

Movie magazines of
the 1930's carried back-page advertisements offering a fifteen-
dollar correspondence course on writing "hit popular songs." I
don't recall the exact statement in the ad of the money to be
earned, but it was well beyond the dreams of avarice and substantial enough to lift the possessor of the secrets right off a Depression breadline. The ads caught my eye because I wanted to write
hits. The fact that I couldn't play a musical instrument did not dis-
courage me. I aspired to be a lyricist like Lorenz Hart or Ira
Gershwin or even Cole Porter. I had played over and over my 78
rpm Brunswick of Ethel Merman belting out "You're the Top." I
wrote two verses in the Cole Porter style. Friends told me I had

talent. Despite this, I had sense enough not to send the money. But I never doubted that there were secrets and that those who were in the know were turning out the hits.

Now some sixty years later I have learned there are no secrets. I learned this by reading the biographies of Irving Berlin, George Gershwin, Vernon Duke, and other songwriters. I learned it again by reading William McBrien's heavyweight biography of Cole Porter. McBrien tells us everything there is to tell about Cole Porter. But no secrets of what it is that makes a hit.

The author of *Tin Pan Alley*, Isaac Goldberg, put it this way: It is relatively simple to explain a hit after it has been made. For the man who can unerringly pick one before the fact a desk stands ready in every publisher's office, with a salary double that of the national president. Is it the words? Is it the tune? Is it the mood? Does the public prefer sad sentiment to happy? Theories have been advanced by every important figure in the business, but the answer remains as much in doubt as ever. Popular taste is at the mercy of whim.

After-the-fact stories about how song hits came into being are unreliable. James T. Maher, in his bouncy introduction to Alec Wilder's *American Popular Song—1900–1950,* says that the history of popular hit songs "has been largely history-by-anecdote. Tales— true, false, altered, benign, malicious, witty, and dull—cling to popular songs like precious gems to a medieval reliquary."

One of these stories reported that Irving Berlin stole his best melodies from the shoe-shine boy in front of the Brill Building where many songwriters kept small offices. The story goes that the shoe-shine boy hummed to himself while putting the final buff on the Berlin wing tips. Irving Berlin picked up the shoe-shine boy's hum and kept humming it on the elevator and then into an office where a musical stenographer stood by to convert the morning's hum into songs such as "Blue Skies" and "A Pretty Girl Is Like a Melody."

This story found its way into print. Billy Rose, a part-time lyricist ("Me and My Shadow," "Don't Bring Lulu") and a big-time Broadway producer, published under his name a New York/ Broadway newspaper column in the 1940's. The column was ghosted by a talented writer. The ghost put a twist on the widespread suspicion that Billy Rose could write nothing but a promissory note. The ghost used the Billy Rose column to retell the Irving Berlin story. He then added that Irving Berlin compensated the shoe-shine boy by paying for an education at Princeton. Now the boy is writing the Billy Rose columns.

What does a biographer do when he discovers he cannot get at what it is that explains the mind of the writer of popular song hits? What does he do when he learns that the songwriter, himself, had no confidence in his own ability to predict whether a song he wrote would be a hit or a flop? What he does is explore in great detail the songwriter's personal life. What turns up is generally unfavorable. Joan Peyser's biography of George Gershwin portrays Gershwin as a rather nasty young man with a disorderly personal life who fathered an illegitimate child. Laurence Bergreen's biography of Irving Berlin portrays Berlin as selfish, insecure, and envious of other songwriters.

McBrien wants to be good to Cole Porter. He is discreet in his revealing that the inspiration for Cole Porter's love-song lyrics follows the line of Marcel Proust's heartbreak relationship with Albertine. The cast of characters McBrien brings in who made up

Cole Porter's circle includes people Proust would have found of interest—for any number of reasons. The names I scooped out at random from the McBrien index have the ring of those in attendance at a Guermantes salon. There is Princess Helen of Roumania, King George II of Greece, the Duc de Tallyrand, the Princess de Polignac, the Duke of Alba, King Alfonso XIII of Spain, Princess Mdivani and, of course, the Duke and Duchess of Windsor.

Cole Porter and his circle reveled in conspicuous consumption. They believed with religious conviction that common decency required them to possess inherited wealth.

How did the boy born on a farm in Peru, Indiana, in 1891 (or as he sometimes said, 1892 or 1893) grow up and connect with such a high-society crowd? The answer is ready cash and a talent to amuse.

That talent accompanied him from Worcester Academy, to Yale and to Harvard Law School. Along the way he picked up a respectable musical education. He dropped out of Harvard Law School and proceeded moderato by small steps to his real port of call, the Broadway musical.

But first World War I. Exactly what he did Over There remains the subject of controversy. He told stories of volunteering as a combat ambulance driver. Some said he got lost on the way to the front, took a wrong turn and wound up on the Champs Elysee in a uniform that startled by its originality those in the regular military.

After the war he played the playboy who wanted to prove that his *saloniste* entertainments, his party songs and lyrics, were up to the Tin Pan Alley requirements—big sheet-music sales. He proved that in 1919. His song, "Old Fashioned Garden," sold very well.

In addition to his songwriting success, in 1919 he had another success. He married Linda Thomas. She was an incontestable beauty, underwritten by millions by way of a divorce settlement. She liked jewelry, especially diamonds as big as the Ritz. Linda's money, Cole's family money, and the royalties that were to roll in put their marriage on a sound financial basis. There was money for travel in oriental splendor to London, Paris, Cairo, and Venice. There were penthouses and villas and white-gloved servants. There was room service, butlers, enablers, and chauffeurs. Mr. McBrien includes photographs of the playful crowd out to prove the theory of the leisure class. The distinguishing characteristic that sets Cole Porter off from his friends was his instinct for workmanship. When he got an offer to write a show he jumped ship, even if it was a yacht. He imprisoned himself in the Waldorf Towers, all pent up in his penthouse, working away on the words and music.

By the time Cole Porter came along, American popular music had undergone many changes. George M. Cohan uncoupled it from bathetic ballads and European operetta. Cohan tricked out his songs with New York slang and catchy titles. This, plus the ragtime craze of the 1900's, assisted by Irving Berlin's "Alexander's Ragtime Band," converted popular music into a highly profitable industry that exported its product worldwide. Its center was New York City where the songwriters, the music publishers, the song-sheet printers, and the song pluggers huddled together rhyming June with Moon under a cloud of cigar smoke. The songs followed a simple musical formula and everything had to be over in three minutes, record time.

Irving Berlin sensed each change in the public's mood. He wrote the best ballads and the best rags. He could do the sophisticated songs that became the 1920's/1930's style, such as "Top Hat,

White Tie and Tails." As the 1920's ended, George Gershwin pulled neck and neck with Irving Berlin. Then Cole Porter gained on them both and won the race.

Why did he win? His knowledge of upper-class superficiality was the real turtle soup. Irving Berlin's and the Gershwins' was only the mock. The ironic language of the upper classes was Cole Porter's mother tongue. The Berlin/Gershwin lyrics reflected the give-away accent of New York's Lower East Side. Cole Porter put into his lyrics the right brand names. He knew them well enough to knock them off. He knew why "Miss Otis Regrets She's Unable to Lunch Today."

By the year 1937, when Cole Porter was 46 years old, the gods themselves grew envious of this man who had it all—the money, the talent, the friends. The gods, thus challenged, struck with a vengeance. Cole Porter was thrown from a horse and suffered serious and permanent leg injuries. He never recovered. He was rarely without pain for the rest of his life. He never again walked without help—a cane, a crutch, a helping hand. And finally the wheelchair.

Despite it all, he continued to write the words and music that conveyed the anguish, not of an injured man, but of the lives of the people who had it all, including the condiment of *weltshmerz*.

McBrien falls into the trap of imposing a heavy analysis on the Cole Porter lyrics. This is a vain endeavor. The lyrics without the music are only light verse that, as light verse, does not get under the skin. It is the words plus the music that do it. Cole Porter's pal, Noel Coward, caught it when he had one of his characters say "Strange how potent cheap music is."

There are two book-long studies of popular song lyrics. The books are *Poets of Tin Pan Alley* by Philip Furia and *Word Crazy* by Thomas S. Hischak. In both books Cole Porter's lyrics are scanned, annotated, and sourced. In neither book can the author give the kick that comes when the lyric dances cheek to cheek with the melody. It is the difference between the lightning bug and the lightning flash. It is the voodoo that Cole Porter does so well.

There is a songwriter's math comparing lyric to melody:

Good lyric + bad tune = no sale

Bad lyric + good tune = good sales

Cole Porter lyric + Cole Porter tune = great sales

Frank Fay, a vaudeville comedian, used the bad lyric-good tune equation to demonstrate how a good tune saves a bad lyric. He used the 1930's popular song, "My Old Flame." He sang the opening line. *My old flame I can't even remember her name.* He satirized the inanity of it. He wound up his monologue by singing, with great emotion, a song of his own called "I Shall Never Forget What's Her Name."

For those who wish to know each detail of Cole Porter's life, McBrien's book is the place to go. Each show and movie is described and each song given its time, place, and circumstances. For those who wish to make believe they have a butler, a porter, and an upstairs maid and can dance like Astaire and Rogers and who want to cure a slightly broken heart by demonizing that old devil called love, I have a prescription. I prescribe an hour with the Cole Porter songs recited by his favorites Ethel Merman and Fred Astaire. When asked why he liked Ethel Merman, Cole Porter said she was the missing link between Lilly Pons and Mae West. As for Fred Astaire, Cole Porter wrote the songs Fred would write if Fred could songwrite as he tap-danced.

My Cole Porter favorites are: "You're the Top," "Just One of Those Things" (written overnight), "Let's Be Buddies," "Anything

Goes," "My Heart Belongs to Daddy," and we'll end with "Make It Another Old Fashioned, Please."

Yes, despite the fact that the times Cole Porter's songs bring back never existed, we shall mark it off as Just One of Those Things. It is the unsubstantial pageant faded, leaving only the songs behind.

Mr. McBrien deals gently with Cole Porter's sad last years. They were days and nights of crowds without company, and dissipation without pleasure. He died in Santa Monica, California, on October 15, 1964.

The American Scholar

AN EVENING WITH
LOUIS ARMSTRONG

I n the late 1950's, Doc Pressman's Randolph Pharmacy, located at 14th and Randolph streets in Washington, D.C., was a meeting place for a number of musicians. There were the locals, Jack "Jive" Schaffer, Roger Calloway, and Buddy Garrison, and also well-known jazz musicians who would occasionally drop in when they were in town. Doc Pressman was both proprietor and pharmacist in residence. He could be found behind a counter at the back of the store. There he was comfortable among his shelves containing thousands of pharmaceutical potions, drugs, vitamin pills, retorts, and odd-shaped glass containers. Doc believed in the therapeutic efficacy of vitamin pills, especially of vitamin E, which he believed, when taken every day in huge quantities, would cure anything. Whether Doc made an independent study or whether the salesman for Hance Bros. vitamin company brought this knowledge to his attention is now unknown and beyond the reach of further research. He was always busy and cheerful. He moved pills very rapidly into small containers. He typed out labels. He actually prepared ointments from the original elements.

Doc, although licensed only as a pharmacist, drifted into the casual practice of medicine by treating a constituency suspicious of orthodox diagnostic techniques. Doc relied heavily on the *Merck Manual,* drug company handouts, hatha yoga, and Ouspensky's *In Search of the Miraculous.* Doc's musician clientele required a pharmacopoeia to help them stay up all night and remain awake all day. (Winston Churchill's physician, Lord Moran, wrote of a somewhat similar problem that Churchill had—he required pills to go to sleep and pills to stay awake.)

Doc purchased one of the first tape recorders manufactured after the war, and he committed his large jazz collection to tape. The tapes played continuously in the back of the store. Doc's favorite was Louis Armstrong's "Satch Plays Fats," the Louis Armstrong recording of Fats Waller songs.

Doc tacked to his small, cork bulletin board postcards from musician friends. Among the cards were several from Louis Armstrong containing affirmations of the remarkable qualities of vitamin E and evaluations of laxative samples that Doc had supplied for him.

One late afternoon in 1955, in the middle of June, Doc said in a casual way that I was to come along with him to meet Louis Armstrong, who was performing at an open-air theater in Washington that advertised itself as providing music "by the stars under the stars." Doc said he had word that "Pops" was running low and needed his medicine cabinet restocked. Doc filled a satchel with vitamin E, vitamin C, and assorted other pills and laxative samples, and I was actually on my way to meet one of the few men who had gained lasting worldwide fame according to the precise terms he had chosen for himself.

We arrived early at the theater and found our way to the dressing-room area. There was no security. We heard the sound of warm-up music as we wandered around asking questions until we found Louis Armstrong's dressing room. I was apprehensive that Doc didn't know Louis Armstrong as well as he made it appear. Would we be just intruders? Doc knocked on the half-opened door of Louis Armstrong's dressing room. He was seated opposite a small table with a mirror above it. On the table were bottles of various pills, bottles of lotion, and bottles bearing the name Pluto Water. The trumpet was on the table, horn end down. He was wearing a bathrobe. He had a large white handkerchief tied up around his head like a hat. Black-rimmed eyeglasses rested on his forehead. He had not yet put on his pants. His white silk stockings were rolled down to his black shoes. He was carefully dabbing a cotton wad into a lubricant and then applying the cotton to his lips. A tape recorder played. Louis Armstrong, without getting up, gave Doc a warm, friendly, husky-voiced greeting. I saw at once that they were real friends, comfortable and relaxed in each other's company, nothing forced.

There was a general flow of conversation concerning Armstrong's recent goodwill tour under State Department sponsorship. He told a few stories concerning food and accommodations in out-of-the-way places. Doc pulled open the satchel to show the contents. Louis Armstrong looked in at the portable medicine chest with great curiosity and obvious satisfaction.

As we talked, I noticed a young man somewhere between eighteen and twenty years old peeking into the dressing room. He was holding the hand of a pretty young girl. The young man caught Doc's eye, and then Armstrong turned around to see where Doc was looking. He saw the innocent young couple and invited them in. The young man was excited by this sudden turn of events. He told Louis Armstrong how thrilled he was to meet and talk to his favorite musician. Armstrong interrupted and asked how he was feeling. The startled young man replied that he was feeling fine. There followed Armstrong's discourse on the need for a good reliable daily laxative. He strongly recommended Swiss Kriss, the laxative he discovered in Sweden. He gave a handful of samples to the young man and woman and then turned again to dabbing his lips with the cotton swabs. The astonished couple withdrew. Doc and I saw that we should leave also because it was nearing show time.

As we were leaving, Louis Armstrong asked me if there was a song I would like to hear. I mentioned the 1932 recording of "That's My Home." He remembered it. He had not sung the song in years, but he was glad I mentioned it because it gave him a good test to see if he could do what he often said he could do—sing the words of just about all of the hundreds of songs he had ever sung. He said that the band would be plenty surprised to hear him start up "That's My Home," but they were all good fakers and they would be all right. He then asked Doc to give him a ride to the Annapolis Hotel after the show was over. We took seats in the audience to the left of the stage. As the curtain went up the band played "When It's Sleepy Time Down South." Louis Armstrong stretched his arms wide, smiled, and said, in a happy, low musical tone, hitting every syllable, "Good evening, everybody." The concert that followed included old favorites, "Blue Turning Gray Over You," "I'm Confessin'," "I Gotta Right to Sing the Blues," and "Saint James Infirmary Blues."

After an intermission the band returned, and four or five more songs rang out in that clear summer night. Then Louis looked in our direction, gave us a big stage wink, and trumpeted into "That's My Home." He played it through just as he did on my old 78 record. He then paused, took out his jumbo handkerchief, drew it past his lips, and sang both the verse and the refrain. As he finished he looked over at us, smiled triumphantly, and raised the trumpet into the air. It was a magic moment. Thomas Mann described those few persons with the unique power to entertain as the dispensers of the joy of life. It is they who by displaying beautiful lighthearted perfection kindle a precious painful feeling, tinctured with envy and wonder, and who can suggest, just for the moment, that the world is filled with wonderful possibilities. For it is they who produce such stuff as dreams are made on.

There were a few encore numbers and then again the strains of "When It's Sleepy Time Down South." Those of us in the know knew that the entertainment was over—a wonderful evening under the stars.

Doc and I waited outside Louis Armstrong's dressing room. He walked out smiling and said that he was sure glad he knew the words to "That's My Home." I was tempted to remind him of his recording of "I'm a Ding Dong Daddy" where he momentarily forgot the words but then made a quick recovery. In Doc's car he joked about the young couple in his dressing room. But he once again emphasized the importance of a good laxative, and he hoped the boy would try the samples. In his rooms at the Annapolis Hotel he had another tape recorder and dozens of tapes. He put on a tape of one of his concerts. He remarked how nice it would be to take a swim on a hot night like this. Doc asked if he was a good swimmer. Yes, he said, he was. It was easy to believe. He had an athlete's build and elegant posture.

Doc and Louis exchanged views on musicians, all diseases curable by patent medicines, Pluto Water, Jergens Lotion for the lips, vitamins, and tape recorders. In conversation, Louis Armstrong was much as he was on stage. He used his enormous range of facial expressions as punctuation. If he said something ironic, he rolled his eyes. If he said something a bit pretentious, he struck a pose of mock seriousness and then growled out deep-throated laughter. He sprinkled musicians' slang into his conversation and used affectionate nicknames for his friends. Doc was Pops. Despite his having just given a two-hour performance, he was filled with a playful energetic enthusiasm for each subject that came up.

The quality of Louis Armstrong's conversation has been the subject of testimony by a number of witnesses. Tallulah Bankhead said of it: "He uses words like he strings notes together—artistically and vividly." His slang, first picked up by musicians, turned up everywhere. He occasionally wrote an article about musicians' slang. After an hour or two, Doc stood up suddenly and announced that we were leaving. It was past two in the morning. Louis Armstrong wrote out a list of the pharmaceutical supplies he needed and told Doc where to send them.

During the ride home, Doc said he often thought of selling his drugstore and signing on as Louis's personal pharmacist. Doc did sell the store a few years later, but he did not travel with Louis Armstrong. He should have. Instead, he drove out to Las Vegas where the Washington, D.C., trumpet player Jack "Jive" Schaffer was making a good living at the Golden Nugget impersonating Louis Armstrong. Doc remained in Las Vegas several months. He must have spent lots of money. When he returned, I could see that he was uneasy without the drugstore. Doc had no family, and the old-timers in the store were his family substitute. No store, no family. Also, Doc was a born salesman. No store, no customers. He also missed his medical practice.

Doc's interest in the metaphysical brought him to Yoga religious services. He learned to sit in the full lotus position. He believed that he was in contact with supernatural forces and that reincarnation was the logical explanation of life's haphazard distribution of misfortune, health, wealth, and sickness. When he withdrew from this earthly existence, he intended to return as a seagull jumping around the beach in Atlantic City, preferably near a cabana at the north end of the boardwalk. Doc's friends could see that he was not doing well. He was even heard to question the therapeutic value of vitamin E.

Within six months after Doc's return from Las Vegas, I found that kind, gentle, helpful man dead, all alone in his small apartment. What happened to all his tapes and those postcards sent to him by the musicians? They had all disappeared.

When I picked up Gary Giddins's 1988 biography of Louis Armstrong entitled *Satchmo*, I looked for Doc's name in the index. There is no index. Too bad such a good book so lovingly put together has no index. Although the book does not mention Doc, it does have a picture of Louis Armstrong in his dressing room with a big smile on his face, just as Doc and I saw him. Another picture shows the Armstrong collection of pharmaceuticals, including a bottle of Pluto Water and the Jergens Lotion. There are reproductions of several of Armstrong's postcards, just like the ones Doc tacked on the corkboard. Giddins has a few comments on Armstrong's Swiss Kriss evangelism and gives a theory to explain the obsession. He connects it with Armstrong's early life when he could not afford proper food and what he did eat caused digestive problems.

Giddins tries, through words, to describe Louis Armstrong's incomparable trumpet playing and singing. The best Giddins does is fail with honor because words cannot convey the effect of Louis Armstrong's prodigious capacity to entertain. Louis Armstrong was one of the very few entertainers who imitated no one but left behind legions of imitators. Al Jolson (who billed himself as the World's Greatest Entertainer) and George M. Cohan (described as both the Prince of the American Theater and the Man Who Owned Broadway) are in the small circle of unique entertainers. Neither had Louis Armstrong's influence, which continues to affect jazz and jazz musicians. There are two biographies of Jolson and two of Cohan. At my last count, there are ten biographies of Louis Armstrong, and they keep coming. Giddins underlines Louis Armstrong's hold on musicians by quoting Bunny Berigan's statement that all a jazz musician needs when he goes on the road is a toothbrush and a picture of Louis Armstrong.

Giddins describes the work habits of Louis Armstrong during the last twenty years of his life. Those work habits were simple: He worked all the time. Every now and then one of his records became a big hit. "Hello Dolly" was the big hit of 1964, and it brought Louis Armstrong back to all the talk and variety shows. He was always unpredictable and spontaneous. He sprinkled his conversation with his own slang creations and neologisms. By the time things were well under way, he had his host of the moment converted to the "Satchmo" style. His lively intelligence and wit, along with the powerful effect of his personality, created a compelling quality impossible to withstand. Everyone felt qualified to do a very good Louis Armstrong.

In the late 1960s Armstrong fell ill, but he continued to work. He appeared on television shows in New York and Los Angeles despite his many serious illnesses, including heart trouble and ulcers. He celebrated his seventieth birthday at the Newport Jazz Festival and then had to be hospitalized. Despite the hospitalization, his calendar continued to fill up with dates long into the future. He had to cancel his appearances because of a second heart attack that put him back in the hospital. He returned home on May 5, 1971, and made plans to resume his schedule. He died at home, two months later, with plenty of good well-paying work on the books.

He had, as Duke Ellington remarked, been born poor, died rich, and hurt nobody on the way. And his melody lingers on. Just about every recording he made is still in print. "That's My Home" has been moved from the original 78 rpm to an LP, and now it can be found all done up on a compact disc.

The American Scholar

PETER ARNO MEETS SOMERSET MAUGHAM

Maugham was dressed in gray slacks, a tweed jacket, black moccasins, and he wore them with the upperclass Britisher's knack of making even new clothes appear faintly shabby and disreputable. Not that there was ever anything bohemian in Maugham's dress or manner. He always played the part of the reserved, well-to-do, top-drawer Englishman—a type he satirized mercilessly in his stories. Sometimes he wore a monocle.

Th;s is the way Karl G. Pfeiffer, one of Somerset Maugham's biographers, describes Maugham's appearance during a meeting in 1941. There is another 1941 meeting between Maugham and an equally attentive observer of matters of dress and manner: Peter Arno. Maugham had agreed to write an introduction to a collection of Peter Arno's cartoons. Maugham, finding himself in New York City performing odd jobs for the British war effort, arranges the meeting. At the time Maugham is 67 and Peter Arno is 37. There are differences between the two in addition to the 30-year age difference.

Maugham—quite short, odd looking and shy. Peter Arno—six foot four, strikingly handsome and socially in control in his own venue, New York City. Photographs of Peter Arno bring to mind the French movie actor Louis Jourdan.

Yet there are resemblances. They both satirized the well-to-do. Maugham gained entry to the circle he satirized by becoming a successful playwright and novelist. Peter Arno came through the door as a matter of right. He was the son of a well positioned New York judge, Justice Curtis Arnoux Peters. Curtis Arnoux Peters, Jr. unilaterally declared himself to be Peter Arno. Both Maugham and Arno defied a family tradition of pursuing a career in the law.

Both Maugham and Arno inspected the world around them with a perceptive and critical eye. Maugham transferred his findings into his novels. where his fictional characters drawn in the main from life exposed the catalog of human frailty. Peter Arno put his findings into the cartoons published in the *New Yorker* from 1925 until his death at age 64.

Maugham's short introduction begins with the draft of a mental picture of Peter Arno before they were to meet. He has heard that Peter Arno is the best dressed man in New York. Well dressed is he? Maugham thought to himself. When Maugham was young and he had all his literary enterprises moving concentrically with the wheels of fortune, he, too, was well dressed, as well dressed as the London tailors could make him. He even crossed the line between the well dressed and the foppish. Maugham had long since outgrown any desire to be remembered by such superficialities as the clothes he wore.

Maugham then turned his attention to the Peter Arno cartoons themselves, as a body of evidence that would reveal the inner man. Maugham's qualifications as an art critic were impressive. He had spotted the trends and he made money buying and selling.

He identified two social types that recur in the Peter Arno cartoons. First, the large man with the bald head and the white moustache. "He has a dignified presence and the complacent authority of inherited wealth. In England he would be the colonel (retired) of a crack regiment, but since he is American I take him to be the president of a corporation." His closet is the home of dinner jackets, tails, and white ties. Laisséz faire has made him world-weary. But sufficient energy remains to fuel a concupiscent look at the blue-eyed cuties. This dignified gentleman occasionally appears in the presence of his wife. She is wise to him. "For all his riches her husband stands in awe of her."

Maugham identified a second type, the small man whose face reflects bewilderment. Although he, too, has an eye for beauty, he is frustrated at every turn. "He is the romantic to whom romance is irremediably denied. He is not a bank president, he is the friend of presidents; he is not a happy man." Maugham decided that this is the real Arno, lurking behind the cartoons as the artist observer rather than the heavy. It was in this state of mind that Maugham met Peter Arno.

Maugham was taken by surprise. He found Peter Arno well dressed but not in the flamboyant manner—certainly not in the manner of Maugham when Gerald Kelly caught him in oils in top hat, walking stick, and white gloves. In their brief meeting Maugham reports that he found Mr. Arno frank and engaging. There is no record of their having met again.

Maugham used his writer's notebook to record his impressions of the people he met, people who, by way of background and appearance, triggered his interest. Although Peter Arno does not show up in Maugham's writer's notebook, he had the mix of elements and the striking appearance that usually attracted Maugham's restless curiosity.

Peter Arno, after graduating from Hotchkiss, went on to Yale. He was not a good student. He disappointed his father who wanted his son to become a lawyer or a banker. The son's main interest was Tin Pan Alley popular music. He was a three-instrument man, playing the piano, the banjo, and the accordion. He put together a jazz band, the Yale Collegians, and in 1923 dropped out of college. Rudy Vallee played the saxophone and did vocals.

Arno took the Yale Collegians into Gilda Gray's Rendezvous Club featuring the new dance, the Shimmy. Occasionally his band played one of his own songs, "My Heart Is on My Sleeve."

He had no training as an artist, but he had artistic talent. He submitted cartoons to the magazines. As he was trying to decide whether he was a bandleader or a cartoonist he sold a cartoon to a new magazine, the *New Yorker*. The *New Yorker*'s thirty-dollar check converted the bandleader into the cartoonist. In addition to what he earned as a cartoonist he had substantial income from a family trust. This funded the life of a *cheval*, the roulette term that identifies the player backing two numbers on each spin of the wheel. Peter Arno's second bet was café society. He wanted recognition as a playboy, a café society man, a pleasure seeker, a wanderer in the terra incognita of desirable women.

Lucius Beebe, the *New York Herald Tribune*'s café society columnist, described the requirements:

> Everyone had to be able to point to some occupation, achievement, distinction, or even notorious frailty that made identification possible. The person might be a

painter, a press-agent, a lover of uncommon appeal, a film actress, the president of an aviation company, the principal patron of a particular restaurant, a society photographer, a professional hostess, or a night-club promoter. The old generalities of "clubman," "millionaire," "society woman," and "internationally known figure in the world of art and politics," were no longer meaningful, valid, or acceptable.

Peter Arno's tag was "that *New Yorker* cartoonist."

The *New Yorker* magazine had its own nightclub reporter, Lois Long. Brendan Gill recalls her as exceptionally intelligent and good-looking. She had shared a New York apartment with Kay Francis, the actress. Peter Arno and Ms. Long met and married and then divorced. Their romance, their marriage, Ms. Long's pregnancy, the birth of their daughter, and their estrangement were recorded in the gossip columns.

While in Reno getting a divorce from Lois Long, Peter Arno got into a fight with Cornelius Vanderbilt, Jr. Mr. Arno was overly attentive to Mrs. Vanderbilt. The Broadway columnists treated this momentous event with the importance it required. On his return to New York he wrote a play entitled *Here Comes the Bride*, based on his marital experience. It opened, there were bad reviews, and it closed. He then worked in collaboration with Cole Porter on a 1930's musical, *The New Yorkers*. In addition to contributing story ideas he did the scenic artwork. It ran 168 performances and is remembered for the Cole Porter song, "Take Me Back to Manhattan." Last year there was a West Coast revival of *The New Yorkers*.

Arno had well publicized love affairs with the beauties of the moment. These included Brenda Frazier, the 1938 deb of the season. Gioia Diliberto, Ms. Frazier's biographer, gives a snapshot of Peter Arno during his affair with Brenda Frazier. "If Brenda was Queen of Café Society, Peter Arno in those days was king. He was tall and lean, with striking, square-jawed looks. Reporters liked to describe him as 'debonair,' a favored ideal of the time. Arno owned seventeen suits, fourteen pairs of shoes, and three dozen shirts, and was a fixture of the best-dressed lists."

The British movie actress, Madeleine Carroll, after dancing with Peter Arno, declared him to be the wickedest-looking man in New York.

Peter Arno and John Held, Jr. overlapped in the 1920's and 1930's at the *New Yorker*. Held was a trained artist, skilled in watercolors, a demanding medium, and in sculpture. Held's popularity peaked in the 1920's with his collegiate and flapper drawings. Corey Ford put the case for Held: "Fitzgerald christened it [the Twenties] the Jazz Age, but John Held, Jr. set its style and manners. His angular and scantily clad flapper was accepted by scandalized elders as the prototype of modern youth, the symbol of our moral evolution."

Arno's take is of an older group who closed the door on the Jazz Age and ignored the Depression. They got out before the crash. They had grown up. They had lost their hair and gained weight. They dressed for dinner. They lived in a Park Avenue duplex. The men tottered like William Powell and their playmates spoke like Myrna Loy. They believed in the worldly values, power and position, the pleasures of the senses, and the supreme importance of liquidity.

By the early 1930's there was a general recognition that Peter Arno was on to something with his cartoons. Four popular cartoon books of his had been published. Stuart Chase gave a favorable review in the *New York Times*. The *Art News* reported that Peter Arno was the person who "heads the field of contemporary

satirists as easily as Kreisler stands at the top of the Fiddling Heap."
Robert Benchley assigned credit to Peter Arno for helping to free
the cartoon from the handcuffs of he-said and she-said. Arno
edited his captions down to a one-liner.

There were frequent Arno art showings including a 1938
exhibit at Averell Harriman's wife's gallery. Lewis Mumford,
reviewing the show, was taken with "Arno's skill in sweeping a simple wash across a figure to create life and vengeance." The Daumier
influence was noted. The personae reflect postural nuances, the rich
man's lordosis and the matron's kyphosis. The facial expressions
show the burden of years of conspicuous consumption.

A number of the cartoon captions became catchphrases.
There was the cartoon of the plutocrats looking out a brownstone
window to other plutocrats on the street below. The caption:
"We're going to the Translux to hiss Roosevelt." There is the plane
crash and the designer observing the wreckage. The caption: "And
now back to the old drawing board." There is the man of specific
intent with his desirable girlie balanced on the bar stool. The bar-
tender looks on. The caption: "Fill 'er up."

The familiar nightclub scene. The man looking into the eyes
of the loverlee young woman. The caption: "Tell me about yourself—your struggles, your dreams, your telephone number."

The familiar dignified man in white tie, intoxicated and
comatose. He is held up by a friendly policeman and a cabdriver.
They present him to the doorman of a Park Avenue apartment
house. The doorman, dressed like a general, says—"He's not ours.
Try River House."

Dining car of a passenger train. An outraged wealthy club
man with martini glass in hand says to the conductor—"This is a
hell of a way to run a railroad. You call this a dry martini?"

As the thirties closed Arno's career as a cartoonist was an expanding success despite the narrow spectrum within which he worked. Although he did not have the skill at caricature of a Ralph Barton, an Al Hirshfeld, or a Miguel Covarrubias, he had developed a following who looked to him for the distinctive pictorial comment.

I spent an enjoyable afternoon examining Peter Arno originals at the Library of Congress. The chain of events that brought me to the Prints Division of the library goes back to the late 1930's. It was then that I first saw the Peter Arno cartoons in *Esquire*, a magazine I read secondhand. It was much too expensive at fifty cents, U.S.A. and three shillings, Great Britain. No one I knew had fifty cents or three shillings to spend on a magazine. The copies I saw were in the barbershop. *Esquire,* in those days, represented the erotic. It was included in barbershop literature along with the *Police Gazette* and *Film Fun.* I also recall seeing a picture in *Life* or *Look* magazine of Peter Arno and Brenda Frazier. Peter Arno represented a life of achievement. He had talent as a cartoonist, he had money, he was handsome, and he lived in New York City. What else could a man ask for? These thoughts remained in my mind, undisturbed, for 50 years or more. I then became friendly with a man who knew Peter Arno and Lois Long. He told me of meeting Lois Long on Fifth Avenue. He spoke to her and then became aware that she had lost most of her eyesight. She recognized him mainly by his voice.

Then some months ago, I ran across the Somerset Maugham article concerning Peter Arno. My curiosity was revived. And here I was, on a rainy Thursday afternoon when I should have been tending to business in my office, turning over Peter Arno cartoons.

Each cartoon was much larger than the published version. The India ink, the wash, the five shades of gray, the highlights in opaque white deliver a tactile sense of the skill of the artist in suggesting that the drawing was an offhand burst of spontaneity. In his foreword to a collection of his cartoons published in 1951 Peter Arno tells how he brought a cartoon to life. The ideas are produced "with blood, sweat, brain-racking toil, the help of the *New Yorker* art staff, and the collaboration of keen-eyed undercover operatives.

"Often it takes days and weeks of patient tearing apart and rebuilding of an idea before the artist is ready to start work." Once he has the idea he makes a sketch in charcoal. He may work 24- or 36-hour sessions, straight through. He dips a fine-pointed sable brush into the India ink. He lays in the heavy black strokes. He wants the look of spontaneity. "You move fast, with immense nervous tension, encouraging the accidentals that will add flavor to the finished drawing." He plays fast and loose, laying on the washes "with careless care, so that it doesn't look like work."

When he is sure he has it he settles back in a deep armchair and stares at it, "even though dawn is breaking in the street outside and your eyes are burning in your head with fatigue; and you gaze on it with a loving joy, and you say to yourself, with a bit of surprise, "By golly, I made it!"

Despite Peter Arno's success as a cartoonist his personal life, as middle age settled in, was another matter. There were two failed marriages. He drank heavily. His playboy pals were dropping out with their own failed marriages and their drinking problems. The nightclub days were going out of style. Sherman Billingsley of the Stork Club had been exposed by Fred Allen as a man who could not say hello without a TelePrompTer.

If Peter Arno had reflected on his playboy years he could have drawn comfort from Somerset Maugham's *The Summing Up*. Maugham believed in the pursuit of pleasure for pleasure's sake.

The spirit is often most free when the body is satiated with pleasure; indeed, sometimes the stars shine more brightly seen from the gutter than from the hilltop. The keenest pleasure to which the body is susceptible is that of sexual congress. I have known men who gave up their whole lives to this; they are grown old now, but I have noticed, not without surprise, that they look upon them as well spent.

I spent two years practicing law with a friend who was a part-time lawyer and a full-time explorer of womanhood. He often said that love was better the second time around. And much more expensive. A new wealthy client did not give him the excitement a new romance did. He was threatened by jealous husbands and by bill collectors, but he thought it a reasonable price to pay for what he had enjoyed and suffered. How did it all end? He lost his law practice, his family, and most friends. But he never regretted, as he put it, "the great work" he had done.

Most who write recollections of the early *New Yorker* magazine days give Peter Arno only a mention, and they are neutral concerning character testimony. There is an occasional comment that he had his dark side. He chose not to become a member of the Algonquin Round Table. He did not look for nor did he seek friendships among the *New Yorker* regulars. One of the few times Peter Arno attended a *New Yorker* party is described in E. B. White's 1952 letter to James Thurber. He notes that Peter Arno played the piano. "We wrapped the party up at 4:45, but it had a couple of hours of early morning enchantment—the kind of goings on that made you feel that the door would presently open and in would walk Scott and Zelda. Arno, much to my surprise, came early and went the whole route. He drank gin and ginger ale, and did not get drunk."

Brendan Gill attended the same party. He describes it in his book *Here at the New Yorker:*

Among those present was Arno, who had taken the precaution to bring along his own large shakerful of dry martinis. The year was 1952, so Arno must have been forty-eight; to me in my thirties he seemed much older than that, and it may have been the case that my impression was correct and that he was indeed prematurely aged; certainly when he died, in 1968, at the age of sixty-four, he was already an old man. One thought then, sadly, oh, but what an extraordinary young man he must have been! And probably he thought that, too, in the increasing misery and loneliness of his last years.

Peter Arno's art, an art of the moment, turns out to have the golden quality, persistence. It is a personal snapshot, in black and white, of a corner of the 1930's. It has the same charm as Eddie Cantor's "Makin' Whoopee" 78 rpm record. It is a corner where the obligatory artifacts are Fred and Ginger, and Nick and Nora. Cole is playing "You're the Top" and adding the fifty-sixth couplet:

You're the top!
You're a sketch by Arno,
You're the top!
You're a Grand Piarno,
Underneath the keys, it's your knees that start to knock,
You're a Palm Beach Party,
You're a New York Smarty,
You're Baby Doc.

You're the top!
You're Kentucky Bourbon,
You're the top!
You're Deanna's Durbin,
I'm a poor imitation of Mr. P's creation,
A flop.
But if Baby, I'm the bottom,
You're the top!

Add to the exhibit Peter Arno's former vocalist, Rudy Vallee, in his shawl-collar tux singing in upper-class accents, "Brother Can You Spare a Dime?" And, of course, a poster-size copy of the "hiss Roosevelt" cartoon.

Arno's last years were reclusive. He left New York City and took up residence in Harrison, New York. His only connection with his New York City days were telephone calls to the *New Yorker* magazine's art director. Arno's last cartoon appeared in the *New Yorker* within a week of his death in 1968. Charles Saxon described it this way. "It was a picture of a nymph reclining in the forest who says to a fawn prancing by, 'Why don't you grow up?' It was Arno at his blithe best, and a beautiful drawing."

In September 1980, the Cartoon Museum located in Port Chester, New York, devoted a special exhibit to Peter Arno. There will be other exhibits and with the passage of time the people who appear in the cartoons will become as interesting as Daumier's witnesses, lawyers, and judges, human still lifes of another time.

The American Scholar

THE EPONYMOUS
MR. PONZI

Hardly a day passes without the Securities and Exchange Commission or some defrauded party filing a pleading charging a defendant with engaging in a Ponzi scheme.

I asked the drafter of one such pleading what the words "Ponzi scheme" meant or contributed to the short and plain statement of the claim showing that the pleader is entitled to relief. No satisfactory answer and no idea who Ponzi was.

Last week I saw the eponymous Mr. Ponzi's name appear in three different newspaper stories. This triggered the recollection that many years ago I had in hand Ponzi's autobiography. With no hope of success in locating the copy again, I turned to the never-failing assistance of The Congressional Library, and Ponzi's book was in hand again. Ponzi published it himself in 1935, some 15 years after his plea of guilty to mail fraud.

The most interesting events in the story commence in 1919, when Ponzi found himself in Boston in a one-room office, with no prospects and no money. In his wanderings he had picked up knowledge of the export-import business and differences in currency rates. He discovered that postage rates and currency rates opened an opportunity to make money on a differential that occurred because of a drop in the value of foreign currency. He had no money to exploit his discovery. But he had imagination. He immediately formed a company to act as the investing agent. He named the company the Securities Exchange Company, the first appearance of the SEC. He then deputized acquaintances to spread the word that people who lent him money would be repaid with a 50 percent return within 45 days. He had notes printed in the name of the company. Ponzi's calculations led him to believe that he could earn enough on the postage differential to make the repayment as promised and still take money off the top for himself.

The money flowed in so fast he hardly knew what to do with it. It became apparent he could not deal with such large sums in accordance with his original plan. He had tapped a Niagara of greed that picked him up and carried him forward despite his occasional desire to arrest it. He had discovered there was no limit to the number of people ready to risk the necessary in order to obtain the superfluous. Thus, the Ponzi scheme was born. It is summarized in *In re Ponzi*, 268 F. 997:

> While Mr. Ponzi is not to be classed in the same category with a robber and burglar, he was undoubtedly a clever manipulator, who took advantage of the credulity of the investing public, which in this instance is the usurer. The investors loaned their money for a

return of the principal and 50 per cent interest [and] would seem themselves to be guilty of usury, if such existed. That Mr. Ponzi took advantage of a weakness and willingness of the community to be victimized is apparent, and sufficient to condemn his acts. So long as the current of money continued to flow in, he could pay the first investors with the receipts from the latter. It was another instance of robbing Peter to pay Paul, of which the past affords examples.

The money came in so fast that he opened branches. He bought banks. He bought the Hanover Trust Company, the Lawrence, Massachusetts Trust Company and large shares in the South Trust Company, the Fidelity Trust Company, and the Tremont Trust Company.

In July of 1920 Ponzi's scheme reached its peak. The main office of the Securities Exchange Company was mobbed with people anxious to give Ponzi their money based on his promise of a 50 percent return in 45 days. Here is the way he describes one unforgettable Boston morning in front of his office:

The air was tense with ill-suppressed excitement. Hope and greed could be read in everybody's countenance. Wads of money nervously clutched and waived by thousands of outstretched fists! Madness, money madness, the worst kind of madness, was reflected in everybody's eyes! In a silent exhibition of utter disdain to all principles of calm and careful judgment. In a silent exhibition of reckless mob psychology, entirely too susceptible to the fatal spell of misguided or perverted leadership!

On that Monday morning in July his cash receipts were one million dollars in three hours. By August he controlled fifteen million dollars and he was under investigation by the postal authorities and the United States attorney. On November 1, 1920, he entered a plea of guilty to mail fraud. Despite the eloquent allocation of counsel, Ponzi received five years.

Ponzi's autobiography gives evidence that he was its actual author. It demonstrates a healthy sense of humor concerning Ponzi's exploitation of the greed he found in the Boston area circa 1920. Most knaves I have known and represented take themselves quite seriously and swear by their own credibility. If challenged they are belligerent and indignant. They deny themselves the cream of the jest, the humor that often attends the transaction involving fraud rubbing against greed. Ponzi knew himself to be a trickster, and he took an artist's delight in dishonesty, which was his form of creation.

Ponzi died at age 66, penniless, in the charity ward of a Rio de Janeiro hospital, on January 15, 1949. A picture of him, taken shortly before his death, shows the confident smile of the former CEO of the Securities Exchange Company. Perhaps the smile was related to a belief that, in years he would not see, the name Ponzi would live as shorthand for schemes to make one rich beyond the dreams of avarice.

WRITING LIKE OLIVER
WENDELL HOLMES

I cannot pass the window of an antique shop that has old fountain pens in the window without going inside to see whether the pens really work. If there is one I like and the price is right, I am in danger of buying it.

Why would anyone have such an interest in old fountain pens? I have no decisive answer to the question. In my case it may be a desire to get even with those days when I wanted a good fountain pen, a Parker or a fancy Waterman, and I did not have the money to buy it. I only had fifteen cents to spend in the five and ten cent store that carried Wearevers, which leaked all over my hands and into my pocket.

Fountain pens were pushed aside by the disposable ballpoints and felt points that flooded the market in the late 1940's. In the last fifteen years fountain pens returned and Waterman and Parker and Montblanc do a good business.

A year ago a pen caught my eye in a Boston antique shop. The fountain pen was old but well preserved. When I asked to see the pen, it was brought from the window display case and placed carefully on a square of green velvet. I unscrewed the cap and held the point up to the light. Each of the two divisions of the pen were even and in line. The nib was in good order. The salesman pointed out that the pen had been given a new valve and ink chamber and could be used for everyday writing. I turned the barrel in my fingers as one would a fine Havana cigar. When I did, I noticed initials on the pen. I held the pen a little closer to see if I could read the initials. When I did this, the salesman said: "You see the initials." I said, "Yes, but I can hardly make them out."

He became confidential and lowered his voice. "Do you know whose initials they are?"

"No, whose are they?"

"Those are the initials of a famous judge."

I said, "The initials seem to be OWH. Are those the initials of Oliver Wendell Holmes?"

"That was the Justice's pen," said the dealer.

He had me. We talked price for a while and then I bought the pen. I asked if there were other things he could show me that had belonged to OWH. He said the other things had been sold. He put the pen in tissue paper, placed it in a small box, and handed it to me, and out I went into the street with a most interesting possession.

I have the two-volume set of Holmes's letters to Sir Frederick Pollock. When I arrived home I took down the books. I drew ink into the pen. I turned to the Holmes letter dated October 13, 1921, in Volume II of the Holmes-Pollock letters. It is on Supreme Court stationery. Holmes refers to Frederick Pollock's letter of September 26, 1921. In that letter Pollock teases Justice Holmes about his handwriting. Pollock says the endings of some of OWH's words require special attention to decipher. Pollock also suggests that OWH's script is a bit too studied and elegant. OWH was proud of his penmanship. In his letter to Pollock OWH defends his penmanship. He rejects the implication that time spent on trifles such as penmanship could be better spent on substantive matters. OWH's guiding principle was that whatever one does must be done well.

I wondered whether Holmes was right-handed or was left-handed, as I am. With a little practice I wrote a few words in the elegant Holmes handwriting style. My experiment gave evidence that the pen I held in my hand could very well have been the pen Holmes used to write his October 13, 1921, letter.

Further corroboration was to follow. When I wrote legal memoranda with the pen it would write no redundant phrases. If there was ambiguity in what I was writing the pen refused to move. The pen would write no citation more than ten years old. Whenever I wrote the word "speech" the pen, on its own, wrote "The most stringent protection of free speech would not protect a man in falsely shouting fire in a theater and causing a panic." In writing personal letters the pen was relaxed and informal. The pen resisted personal disclosures. It was comfortable writing about books, philosophy, and the little we can ever know of this puzzling universe in which a man with pen and paper plays such an insignificant role.

Anyone who collects fountain pens is aware that the pen you do not want to lose is the very pen you do lose. And that is what happened to the OWH pen. I attended a meeting where complicated releases and agreements were passed around and signed by lawyers and clients. One of the persons in the signing ceremony kept looking at my OWH pen. I made the mistake of talking about it. I knew when I boasted of my possession that bad luck was to follow.

When the meeting was over I returned to my office. I had letters on my desk to be signed. I reached into my coat pocket for the OWH pen. Not there and not anyplace else. I panicked. I reconstructed where I had been. I made telephone calls. All to no avail.

I am trying to get over the loss of that pen by persuading myself that it was a counterfeit. When next in Boston I will return to the antique shop. Perhaps I will discover that the dealer has an unlimited supply of old pens with OWH scratched into the barrel. But is it really of importance whether it was the real thing or only a fake, whether it was the real turtle soup or only the mock? I had the pleasure of writing a few sentences guided by the spirit of OWH.

I believe I know the person who has the pen. And if that dignified gentleman who was at the meeting when the pen disappeared, the dignified gentleman who kept talking about the full-length Holmes portrait at The Law School, the dignified gentleman who was wearing the dark blue suit and the light brown shoes, if that overly dignified gentleman reads this and the pen is returned, let me say that ends the matter, and no questions asked.

BING CROSBY, GUS EDWARDS, O. HENRY, AND ALIAS JIMMY VALENTINE

T he first volume of Bing Crosby's two-volume biography is in the bookstores. For the youngsters, Bing Crosby (1904–1977) was the Zeitgeist of popular music from the 1930's to the 1960's. The biography's index lists the name of Gus Edwards. Who was he and why is he in Bing's biography? Bing played the part of Gus Edwards, an old vaudevillian and songwriter, in the movie *The Starmaker*. Bing sings the Gus Edwards song, "When Jimmy Valentine Gets Out." Who was Jimmy Valentine and what did he get out of? Jimmy Valentine was a picaresque safecracker who did time. When he got out he intended to crack just one more safe.

Stay with me and I will pull all this together and give you what is called an O. Henry, firecracker ending. William Sydney Porter, alias O. Henry (1862–1910), also did time. He was charged with embezzlement—taking money from a bank in Texas where he worked as a teller. Whether he was guilty or not has never been resolved. Nevertheless, he jumped bond before the trial. His flight was taken as an admission of guilt. See *Illinois v. Wardlow*, 528 U.S. 119 (2000). Flight is the consummate act of evasion and is evidence of wrongdoing. At least so sayeth the majority opinion.

William Sydney Porter and Jimmy Valentine met in jail. When Porter got out he moved to New York and commenced writing short stories under the name O. Henry. One of his stories, "A Retrieved Reformation," told what happened to Jimmy Valentine after he got out. Jimmy intended to go straight after cracking one more safe—an old safe in an old bank in a small town. When he got to the small town, he took a job in a shoe store, not to sell shoes, but as a cover while casing the bank. His due diligence at the bank brought something he did not expect. He met a girl. It was love at first sight for them both. Add to the plot that she was the daughter of the bank president.

The banker took a liking to Jimmy. He decided to give a party at the bank for the two in love. The party served a double purpose: The banker would introduce Jimmy to his friends and he would show off the bank's new time safe.

Jimmy had a lot to think about at that party. He had not planned on falling in love and he had not planned on cracking a time safe. Although Jimmy was amiable at the party, his thoughts were on the two unexpected events.

His girlfriend's sister was at the party with her two young children, who were playing hide-and-seek right in front of the open safe. Then a dramatic event took place. One of the little girls ran into the safe to hide. Another child pushed the safe door and it swung closed. Let's leave the story right there and go back to O. Henry.

The Jimmy Valentine story, as you will see, was a natural to be made into a play. O. Henry was tempted, but he was apprehensive that if the play were successful his double life would be exposed. He liked his O. Henry anonymity. He sold the rights to a playwright for $500, and the story was dramatized and renamed *Alias Jimmy Valentine*. It was a Broadway success and many years later a 1930's movie.

Back to Gus Edwards. He saw the play and it inspired him to write the song "When Jimmy Valentine Gets Out." It was the hit of the 1911 season.

Now back to the bank and the little girl in the safe. The guests at the party who saw what happened cried out. The safe must be opened or the little girl will die. A call was put in to the police and to the people who installed the time safe. The word was that the time safe could not be opened until 24 hours later.

As Jimmy watched this tragedy unfold, he had to make a quick decision. Could he open the safe? And if he could, should he? It would show him up as a safe cracker.

Jimmy's technique with the combination lock tumblers was to sensitize his fingers with some sandpaper. And without thinking any more, he rubbed the tips of his fingers against the adjacent marble wall. He went to the safe. He turned the tumblers. He felt the clicks that revealed the combination. He still had the touch in those sandpapered fingers. Lo and behold, the safe popped open. The little girl danced out, unaware that she just sidestepped death.

Jimmy looked around to see what the reaction was to him. Standing back from the crowd was a man he recognized, a detective from the safe squad who had come over to the bank when the call was made to the police. It was the detective who had put Jimmy in jail two years earlier.

Jimmy walked over to him and said, "You saw it all, and now you must do your duty."

The detective said, "Yes, I saw it all. I thought I recognized you, but I see I have made a big mistake. You are a better man than the man I thought you were."

Let's end with a song—a Gus Edwards song:

Look out, look out, Look out for Jimmy Valentine
For he's a pal of mine, A sentimental crook
With a touch that lingers
In his sandpapered fingers
He can find the combination of your pocketbook.
Look out, look out, For when you see his lantern shine
That's the time to jump right up and shout
Help! He'd steal a horse and cart, He'd even steal a girlie's heart
When Jimmy Valentine gets out.

JOE BORKIN, THURMAN ARNOLD, SUKARNO, AND BRITISH PETROLEUM

I met Joe Borkin in the 1960's when each of us had an office in the Ring Building at 18th and M streets. In talks with Joe I learned he was one of those people who as a young man wanted to read every book in the library. As a by-product of that effort, he knew a lot of things about a lot of people. If someone could not finish a sentence because he couldn't remember a name or the title of a book, Joe quickly supplied what was needed and then he would add the relevant bibliography on the subject in question.

Joe was a man of obsessions. Within his major obsession of wanting to know everything were his minor obsessions, such as the complete works of Sigmund Freud, the complete works of Thorstein Veblen, and John Kenneth Galbraith's theories of why the stock market crashed. Despite these distractions, Joe obtained a degree in economics and took it to the Department of Justice in the late 1930's.

There he met the man who had a decisive influence on his life. The man was Thurman Arnold, who was in charge of reawakening the antitrust division of the Department of Justice. Thurman Arnold has been described as contradictory, dramatic, intriguing, and ironic, and with no desire to clarify the signals. Joe was Thurman Arnold's economic adviser, theoretician, Boswell, server of subpoenas, and the expert on the conspiratorial behavior forbidden by the Sherman Act.

Thurman Arnold's satirical commentaries on government and myth, *Folklore of Capitalism* and *Symbols of Government*, organized Joe's theories of political science.

President Roosevelt in 1943 appointed Thurman Arnold to the United States Court of Appeals for the District of Columbia Circuit. Arnold recalled, "I confidently expected to spend the rest of my life in a position of great dignity, with long vacations in the summer, in an atmosphere where the wicked cease from troubling and the weary are at rest." When Thurman Arnold became Judge Arnold, Joe Borkin left Justice to go out on his own as a consulting economist and writer. When Joe and I met in the 1960's Joe was busy writing the history of the German cartel I.G. Farbin. Joe eventually finished the book and when published it made the best-seller list.

Judge Arnold discovered he did not have the temperament for appellate judging. He wanted to be a player rather than an umpire. "I was impatient with legal precedents that seemed to me to reach an unjust result. I felt restricted by the fact that a judge has no business writing or speaking on controversial subjects. A judge can talk about human liberties, the rule of law above men, and similar abstractions. All of them seemed to me dull subjects."

In the 1950's Indonesia was in turmoil. Competing local armies fought each other when they were not fighting the Dutch colonials. A person who emerged from all the conflict who seemed to hold out the best prospects for Indonesia was, simply, Sukarno. His publicity labeled him as his country's George Washington. Sukarno needed money to fund his troops. He let it be known that he was selling shares in his prospects of victory.

Thurman Arnold made a chance remark to a Sukarno representative that Joe Borkin might have among his wide acquaintance of friends a few people who would like to help Sukarno bring democracy to Indonesia. The chance remark initiated a meeting between Sukarno and Borkin. Borkin took Sukarno's cause to friends in the movie business. One of these people was an erratic genius who made lots of money by signing up Abbott and Costello to make movies. B movies for a B-rated Hollywood studio. This erratic genius bought shares in Sukarno.

In time Sukarno won out and tried to bring order out of disorder in Indonesia. When he came into power, he remembered his friends. He worked out a plan to give the investors shares in certain Indonesian oil wells.

The investors nominated Joe Borkin (who did not invest) to go to London and arrange to meet with the high officials in British Petroleum to sell BP the oil properties. Joe took the deeds and went to London.

Joe described what happened this way. BP's man, Sir Something or Other, invited Joe to a meeting in a leather-bound office. Joe told Sir Something or Other of his mission. He produced the deeds. Sir Something or Other looked at the deeds, examined the seals, examined the signatures. He held the deeds up to the light. He then pressed a button and someone came into the office, and Sir Something or Other said "Charles, look these over and be back here as soon as you can and tell us whether they are authentic."

Charles left and Sir Something or Other offered Joe a Cuban cigar. They talked of London hotels. Sir Something or Other said his favorite was the Stafford.

In a few minutes Charles returned and handed the deeds and a note to Sir Something or Other. Sir Something or Other handed the note to Joe. The note said, "These deeds are authentic."

Joe handed the note back to Sir Something or Other, who then handed the deeds back to Joe. Then Sir Something or Other leaned forward and said to Joe, "I have some good news and some bad news. Joe—do you mind if I call you Joe?—these deeds are authentic. That's the good news. Now the bad news. As long as you have these deeds, your life isn't worth a shilling. Burn them and get out of here as soon as you can."

Joe did exactly as he was told. He returned home with the bad news. The investors had prepared a gift for Joe that they intended to present to him to commemorate his triumphant return. After Joe spoke they understood that they were childishly shortsighted in their expectations of wealth beyond the dreams of avarice.

The gift was a fine portrait of Thurman Arnold done by an Indonesian artist of some fame. As years went by, the portrait, on display in Joe's office, was Joe's reminder of those exciting Sukarno days ending with Joe's trip to London.

COHAN AND HARRIS
AND THE LAW OF BEING
ON THE SQUARE

Come with me to an antique furniture store on University Place in Greenwich Village. As we enter we are greeted by the proprietor. We tell him we would like to see an old-fashioned partners desk. He just happens to have such a desk. They are very rare and very expensive when in good condition. The one he has is in excellent condition. He takes us to an ornate desk that is two desks in one. Each side is a complete desk with a kneehole for each partner and an identical stack of desk drawers on each side.

He asks what we know about partners desks. Without waiting for an answer, he says that when this particular desk was in use, probably around 1910, the partners faced each other across the desk.

He asks whether we ever heard of George M. Cohan. Of course we have heard of George M. Cohan. He was the Prince of the American Theater. He did everything. He wrote songs and plays. He wrote "Give My Regards to Broadway" and "Over

There." He was a dancer. He was an accomplished actor. The movie *Yankee Doodle Dandy* is about him, with Jimmy Cagney playing George M.

He then says: "Did you know who his partner was?" As a matter of fact, we do. His name was Sam Harris. "Why are you bringing up George M. Cohan's name?"

"I have reason to believe this is the desk that Cohan and Harris used when they were partners."

I want proof. "What gives you reason to believe this was the Cohan and Harris desk?"

"In the desk drawers were letters addressed to Cohan and Harris. On this side there was a ledger book of accounts of the partnership and on the other side were notes—not promissory notes but musical notes. That was Cohan's side. Harris, as the businessman, sat on the other side."

When partners conducted business face to face, they used a big book to record the letters received and a daily log of partnership affairs. A ledger recorded the disbursements and receipts. Cash, checks, and contracts were kept in a big safe in the corner of the room. Each partner's name was written on the safe in bold fancy gold leaf, followed by the word *Partner*.

Cohan, years after his retirement, reminisced with friends about his commencement of the Cohan and Harris handshake partnership:

> This Harris man, by the way, is a very surprising person [pointing to Harris]. Full of surprises. I know he's handed me many a surprise. I don't mean by that that I didn't know he was always a great showman—a great judge of plays, and all that sort of thing, but I mean really he's a surprising man. I remember the first time

he surprised me. Of course when Sam and I went into business together, I naturally thought he had a lot of money. We didn't talk about that until we were in the middle of rehearsals for our first show, and then when he told me he was broke, that was my first surprise. And he seemed to be just as much surprised as I was when I told him I was broke too! And the members of the company were very much surprised when they found out we were both broke!

Some law partnerships have a similar beginning. Each partner expected the other partner to bring in the business. On the recoil one partner returns to the government and the other joins up with a firm that has prospects.

Cohan liked to say that Harris and he were always on the square with each other. Judge (later Justice) Cardozo translated "always on the square" into baroque legalese:

> ... copartners, owe to one another, while the enterprise continues, the duty of the finest loyalty. Many forms of conduct permissible in a workaday world for those acting at arm's length, are forbidden to those bound by fiduciary ties. A trustee is held to something stricter than the morals of the market place. Not honesty alone, but the punctilio of an honor the most sensitive, is then the standard of behavior. As to this there has developed a tradition that is unbending and inveterate. Uncompromising rigidity has been the attitude of courts of equity when petitioned to undermine the rule of undivided loyalty by the "disintegrating erosion" of particular exceptions. ... Only thus has the level of conduct

for fiduciaries been kept at a level higher than that trodden by the crowd. It will not consciously be lowered by any judgment of this court. *Meinhard v. Salmon,* 164 N.E. 545 (1928).

Cohan and Harris were successful in putting on George M.'s musical shows and in buying theater properties. Nevertheless, the partnership split up. Cohan objected to actors in his plays joining unions. Harris saw unions as inevitable. They ended the partnership but remained good friends. Not only did they want to, they had to. They married sisters.

What if Cohan and Harris had found themselves in litigation over the conduct of the partnership? If they had, they would get little help from the law as it then existed. Much of the uncertainty was due to a bitter conflict in legal theory between the entities and the aggregates. The entity true believers declared that a partnership was a transcendental entity with a soul and existence of its own independent of the partners of the moment. The aggregate true believers declared that a partnership was a snapshot of the partners at a given moment. Each time a new partner joins up or an old partner leaves there is, by law, a dissolution.

What was needed was an edict from an authoritative priesthood. The edict was delivered in 1914 by the Conference of Commissioners on Uniform State Laws. It was in the form of the Uniform Partnership Act and it declared the aggregates the winner. But as with so many disputes between fanatics, the losers went to the hills and waged common-law guerrilla warfare.

ROSA LEWIS, THE OLD CAVENDISH, AND TAKING THE FIFTH

Accompanying a client who must assert Fifth Amendment rights before a grand jury is not an occasion conducive to good conversation. Both the lawyer and the client are concerned as to just how things will go. The client will be under oath and warned that perjury is a felony. This, itself, is unpleasant. Add that the client may be a respectable businessman who is embarrassed by having to refuse to answer on the grounds that his answers may tend to incriminate.

I try to avoid those hours of stilted conversation when traveling with a client to out-of-town federal courts. Therefore if the client and I are in different cities, I suggest each finds his own method of travel to the courthouse.

Some years ago I thought I had arranged that I would take the Metroliner alone and do some uninterrupted reading. But then plans changed and we agreed to meet in Washington and take the train up to Philadelphia together. Thus he and I would be together for several hours with little to say. He was a dignified southern gentleman who was not talkative under the best of conditions, and these were not the best conditions.

I decided to make no effort at small talk during the train ride. I brought with me a book about Rosa Lewis (1867–1952), who ran the notorious old Cavendish hotel on Jermyn Street in London. *Masterpiece Theatre* dramatized the goings-on at the hotel in a TV series focusing on Rosa Lewis, and the way she ran the Cavendish as an upper-class honey pot.

She was a former kitchen maid who climbed the ladder of good fortune that led her to the ownership of her own hotel. Lord Ribblesdale and other toffs became semi-permanent guests until things quieted down in their home life.

One of her upper-class clients was the subject of a notorious breach of promise suit. He refused to settle. His love letters were read out in court and printed in the newspapers. He met with his cheerleaders every evening at the Cavendish. He won. Such suits were a danger to Rosa's clientele. The boys got together and used their influence to get a statutory nullification of such claims. It is blackmail, nothing but blackmail.

As we settled into our Metroliner seats I saw that my client had a book. This meant it would not be discourteous for me to read my book. After he read a few pages—it was a best-seller mystery—he put it down.

I read a few pages of my book and then my mind wandered to episodes before grand juries where things did not go as planned. I closed the book and put it on the tray. Then to my surprise this reserved gentleman reached right over and picked up my book. He opened it and looked carefully at the pictures of Rosa Lewis, the lobby of the Cavendish hotel, and the picture of

Evelyn Waugh, who in his novel *Vile Bodies* gave an unflattering portrait of Lewis. Why would a businessman from a small southern town take such an interest in a long-ago disreputable London hotel? When he replaced the book I could see a change in his mood. Some of the tension had left his face.

He asked if I had ever stayed at the Cavendish. I said I had but that was years after the old hotel had been bombed out during World War II. When I was there it was just another commercial hotel. I asked if he'd ever stayed at the Cavendish. He said he had. He was stationed in London during the war and the Cavendish was his home away from home until it was hit by a bomb during the Blitz. He said he knew Rosa Lewis quite well. He even had letters from her.

The next few hours on the train were very pleasant. I learned things about Rosa Lewis that were not in the book. As we talked we momentarily forgot we were on our way to an appointment with a grand jury.

At the courthouse we reported as the subpoena directed to room 2021. We gave our names and within a half hour my client was behind the closed doors of the grand jury room. His instructions were to plead the Fifth as soon as the questions touched on his business dealings. My estimate was he would be out in ten minutes. My estimate was wrong.

As the time passed I worried. Did he decide to answer any question that was asked? Did he wait too long to answer, and did the prosecutor advise him that he had waived the privilege? What was going on in there that was taking so much time?

When the door opened 45 minutes later, he walked out looking pretty good. I asked the Department of Justice man if my client had to return. He said with a smile, only if he was granted immunity.

We cleared out, and as soon as we were on the street I asked what took so long. He said everything went well. He gave his name and address. Then a woman on the grand jury asked a lot of questions about his hometown and the high school and people who lived in the town.

"We had a long chat about changes on Main Street and whether Joe's Coffee Shop is still there. That was all fine, but I was worried that word of my grand jury appearance would find its way back home. That would be embarrassing. So after we concluded our talk about the locals, I asked the prosecutor whether what took place in the grand jury room was secret. He was emphatic in saying that the only person who had a right to disclose what took place was me.

"After that we got around to the Fifth and all went smoothly."

He took his flight back to his home and I boarded the Metroliner. As Samuel Pepys commented in his diary, things have a way of working themselves out.

DR. BERNHARDI

In the process of discarding old files I found two on a client I shall call Dr. Bernhardi. There was nothing memorable in the files, but there is much to be remembered about Dr. Bernhardi. She was from Eastern Europe. She spoke all the languages of the countries through which the swirl of war had carried her before she took up residence in Washington. When we met she was the physician of choice to those in the outermost rings of the Washington diplomatic circle, people whose self-importance was defined by the receipt of an invitation to an embassy social function. Failure to attend a function when invited might lead to the invitee's being stricken from the C list, with no invitations to follow.

But what was to be done if the invitee had laryngitis? What if the invitee had the flu? What if the invitee was recovering from surgery? There was only one thing to do: Call Dr. Bernhardi.

When she got the call, she immediately went to the patient's house. She carried a black satchel filled with quick-fix medical tricks. As she took a brief history, she performed whatever physical examination was necessary, a look here and a tap there. Then came the injections, the pills, the prescriptions, and the placebo effect of Dr. Bernhardi's presence. If the invitee was a woman, Dr. Bernhardi dressed her. If appropriate, she brought in a beautician. In the space of two hours the invitee was out of bed, powdered and painted, and ready to go. Dr. Bernhardi would drive the invitee to the party, escort her to the door, and remain until the invitee advanced to an upholstered chair. In a few hours the doctor would return. In a stage whisper she announced that the invitee's chauffeur had taken ill and the invitee must go home at once to deal with the emergency. Dr. Bernhardi took the invitee back home and put her to bed with hot water bottles, aspirin, electric blankets, and sleeping pills.

Dr. Bernhardi's home was also her office. The building was a 16th Street mansion that had seen better days. Dr. Bernhardi converted it into a safe house for between-assignments headwaiters, butlers, chauffeurs, and cooks.

During one of our conferences, an elderly gentleman required Dr. Bernhardi's services. He was a waiter. On the evening in question he could just as well have been delivered to a funeral parlor as to the embassy party he was working. Dr. Bernhardi worked on him like a prizefighter's second. She whispered words of encouragement as she went through her ministrations. As I watched, there came to mind the joke of the second saying to the bruised and bloodied fighter, "He hasn't laid a glove on you. Get back in there." The fighter replies, "If he hasn't laid a glove on me, keep an eye on the referee. Somebody's pounding me to death in there."

I met Dr. Bernhardi through a friend who obtained a law degree in France, then gained admittance to the local bar. He did legal work for Dr. Bernhardi's patients. Within this group were a few who were fascinated by litigation in our courts. They were astonished to learn that for a filing fee of a few dollars they could set off the entire legal apparatus of clerks, judges, and jurors. In their country of origin, so they said, the law was corrupt and the law's delays interminable. Here they were treated to a system that was honest and reasonably efficient. They wanted the thrill of the trial and the dramatic experience of a jury verdict.

Representing such litigiophiliacs produced repeated frustrations. If the defendant offered $3,000 in settlement against a $5,000 demand, the client would not reduce the demand in accordance with the negotiation tango. The client would raise the demand in order to defeat a settlement. The case must be tried. That is the American way.

I represented Dr. Bernhardi in two lawsuits. She promptly settled both. She was skeptical of what the law had to offer. Her skepticism was based on the wide knowledge of human nature that a physician gains over 40 years of practice. She saw human nature bare, a bundle of contradictory elements that connect and disconnect in an unpredictable way like the colored glass fragments of a kaleidoscope. The lawyer, on the other hand, learns what a client chooses to disclose. The real truth is revealed only after a long trial, if at all.

Dr. Bernhardi put her trust in the empirical such as the circulatory system, the services of reliable unlicensed plumbers and electricians, and an arrangement with a cook with access to the pantry of the French Embassy.

The last time I saw Dr. Bernhardi it was to get her advice concerning my own bad case of laryngitis. She listened to my whispered complaints. She wrote out a prescription for an arcane gargle. Need I say more? It worked. And if I had wanted to celebrate my recovery by attending the party in honor of the new ambassador from Belgravia or the reception for the legal adviser for Puritania, I am sure Dr. Bernhardi would have arranged for the invitation.

CLINTON, ASQUITH, AND SCHOPENHAUER

What do William Jefferson Clinton, Herbert Henry Asquith, and Arthur Schopenhauer have in common? Asquith and Clinton are politicians who, as Disraeli said, reached the very top of the greasy pole to power and both further distinguished themselves in the terra incognita of womanhood. And what of Schopenhauer? We shall see.

H. H. Asquith at the turn of the century epitomized what the British upper class so prized—seemingly effortless accomplishment. He commenced his career as a barrister. His success was immediate. He soon turned to politics and was elected to a seat in the House of Commons. When Asquith was forty-two, he married Margot Tennant. She had contrived to make herself a controversial and much-talked-about figure in English society.

In 1905, Asquith's Liberal party came to power and Asquith was installed as prime minister in 1908. He, as Clinton, had won his way to the top entirely by talent and political achievement. He had neither rank nor wealth to help him along.

Now enter the woman in the case, Venetia Stanley. When Asquith met her, she was 25 and he was 58. She was a very attractive, highly intelligent brunette, surrounded by ardent suitors. Asquith put in writing his thoughts the day he fell in love with Venetia:

> Suddenly, in a single instant ... the scales dropped from my eyes ... and I dimly felt ... not at all understanding it that I had come to a turning point in my life.

Their unique correspondence began in 1910. The letters numbered in the thousands. He wrote as many as three a day. His letters were indiscreet. They continued after World War I was declared. They contained secret information concerning ship and troop movements and strategy decisions. They contained highly personal information about his friends and associates. Asquith gave Venetia his contemporaneous reaction to Asquith's great contemporaries, among them Winston Churchill. In the letter of February 26, 1915, he writes: "Our War Council lasted nearly 2½ hours. Winston was in some ways at his worst—having quite a presentable case. He was noisy, rhetorical, tactless & temperless—or—full."

Asquith was not the only man in Venetia's life. Asquith's close friend and political secretary, Edwin Montagu, was also a suitor. Unknown to Asquith, in letter after letter Montagu pressed Venetia to marry him. She was reluctant to end things with Asquith. She kept Asquith in the dark until she agreed to marry Montagu. On May 12, 1915, she breaks the news. She tells Asquith of her engagement to Montagu. It strikes like a hammer. Asquith writes to Venetia on May 12, 1915:

Most loved—

As you know well, this breaks my heart.
I couldn't bear to come and see you.
I can only pray God to bless you—and help me.

On May 12, 1915, the morning papers carried the news of German atrocities, and the press raised the question of whether Asquith had the resolve to fight an all-out war. Soon David Lloyd George stepped forward and deposed Asquith, who left office never to return. As time went by, he collected a few evening honors. He died in 1928.

Montagu died rather young, at age forty-five. During the nine years of Venetia's marriage, she did not write Asquith, but directly after Montagu's death, Venetia wrote a very touching letter to Asquith and with it the story ends.

My darling Mr. Asquith,

Edwin asked me to give you something of his and I finally thought you might like this *Hamlet* which I'd given him a long time ago. I've never thanked you for your divine letter, you know how dumb and inarticulate I am, but you do realize I hope how glad I was to get it. I hope I may see you sometime when you get back.

Much love always.
Venetia

The question that arises in such cases is whether such a relationship affects the conduct of the office. It is clear it was not the

war that was on Asquith's mind in early May 1915. It would take
quite a man to give his attention to his office when his mind was
filled with love for a spirited young woman, and with the suspicions of his wife, and with the humiliation of seeing his closest
working partner take away the love of his life.

And now Arthur Schopenhauer. His interest in the subject
we are discussing was mostly academic. Nevertheless his insights
are startling. Read in connection with today's news they explain
the unexplainable. Schopenhauer answers the question—How
could he be so dumb? It is not a matter of intelligence. Schopenhauer wrote in 1844 that no matter how sexual love disguises itself
it has

> an unfavourable influence on the most important
> affairs, interrupts every hour the most serious occupa-
> tions and sometimes perplexes for a while even the
> greatest minds. It does not hesitate to intrude with its
> trash, and to interfere with the negotiations of states-
> men and the investigations of the learned. It knows
> how to slip its love notes and ringlets even into minis-
> terial portfolios and philosophical manuscripts. Every-
> day it brews and hatches the worst and most perplex-
> ing quarrels and disputes and destroys the most valuable
> relationships, and breaks the strongest bonds. It
> demands the sacrifice sometimes of life or health,
> sometimes of wealth, position, and happiness. Indeed, it
> robs of all conscience those who were previously hon-
> orable and upright, and makes traitors of those who
> have hitherto been loyal and faithful. Accordingly, it
> appears on the whole as a malevolent demon, striving
> to pervert, to confuse, and to overthrow everything.

One of today's statesmen might find himself right at home in Asquith's war cabinet. To his left would be his leader, H. H. Asquith, writing love letters to Venetia. To his right he would see the Chancellor of the Exchequer, David Lloyd George, a married man, reading a love letter his secretary and mistress, Frances Stevenson, delivered by hand into the Cabinet Room.

GENERAL BUCK LANHAM, ERNEST HEMINGWAY, AND THAT WOMAN IN VENICE

Thereare dull social gatherings where the guests do not know each other and have nothing in common. They wander about, wondering why they were invited and why they accepted the invitation. At such gatherings it is inevitable that conversation is attempted with the question, "What do you do?" When I am asked that question and I say I am a lawyer, I know there will be the follow-up question, "What kind of a lawyer are you?" Then I start fumbling. I don't know what to say. Yesterday, at a deposition in New York, I learned the answer. When the deponent, a lawyer, was asked what kind of law he practices, he said: "I am a Pike lawyer."

"A Pike lawyer? What kind of practice is that?"

"Yes, a Pike lawyer. I take what comes down the Pike."

Some lawyers say they are litigators. I am not up to that. I don't like the sound of the word or some of the words that rhyme with it. I never heard the word until the 1980's. It was then that it was discovered that there is substantial money in litigation. Before that the established firms were wary of trial work. Losing the big case could mean losing a big client. Criminal work was routinely sent out to trial counsel prepared to take the fall.

In the 1980's, what with special prosecutors and asbestos and big-time corporate fraud, both civil and criminal litigation became profit centers, and firms set up litigation sections. Those in the litigation sections referred to themselves as litigators.

At one of those dull social gatherings where nobody knew anybody, I was hit with the inevitable "What kind of lawyer are you?" I started to respond (it was before I learned about the Pike answer), and then I saw that, across the room, my wife was enjoying a conversation with a respectable-looking couple. I disengaged from the pending question and went over to find out who these people were and what they were talking about. I was introduced to Buck and Jane Lanham. The conversation was a humorous discussion of the predicament in which we found ourselves. Buck Lanham said we must make a choice: We could stay and retaliate against the host by overeating and overdrinking, or we could retreat to a good restaurant. We retreated to dinner.

Over dinner we learned that Buck Lanham was retired military. In retirement he was pursuing many interests, including studying French literature, writing poetry and short stories, and raising Swiss chard.

That evening at home, the name Buck Lanham connected in my mind with Ernest Hemingway. The next day I went to the library and took down biographies of Hemingway. They all mentioned Hemingway's close friendship with Lanham, Major General Charles T. Lanham. He was born in Washington, D.C., and graduated from West Point in 1924. Among his many military adventures, he was the infantry officer who commanded the American 22nd Regiment in Normandy in 1944 and led a breakout in the Battle of the Bulge. It was in the Normandy battles that Lanham and Hemingway first met. Hemingway was doing battlefield stories for the American audience. Hemingway described Lanham as "the finest and bravest and most intelligent military commander I have known."

Hemingway liked heroics. One of his critics said, "For Hemingway courage is a permanent element in a tragic formula: Life is a trap in which a man is bound to be beaten and at last destroyed, but he emerges triumphant, in his full stature, if he manages to keep his chin up."

Here is my discussion with Buck Lanham concerning Hemingway's courage hang-up:

J.A.S.: Did you discuss courage with Hemingway?

B.L.: That is all he wanted to talk about. Courage for me was something I happened to be born with. Luck and courage. Without luck, courage often means a short life-expectancy. I told him that a sober person does not discuss courage in public.

J.A.S.: What else did you and Hemingway talk about?

B.L.: I wanted to talk about my short stories. They were good. He was not interested. He wanted to talk about this grace-under-pressure crap.

Lanham received many military decorations for his repeated acts of courage and bravery. Hemingway would have liked to have been Buck Lanham. In fact, Hemingway became Buck Lanham in Hemingway's 1950 novel, *Across the River and Into the Trees*. Venice is the setting. Lanham/Hemingway is the hero using the name

Colonel Richard Cantwell. The colonel was briefly a brigadier general, but was reduced in rank by some incompetents. He is 51 years old and, in the words of the flyleaf, "a man of fierce and embittered pride who is coming too soon to the end of his physical tether. War has scarred and marred his body; his heart in particular shows war's ravages and gives him warnings which he cannot ignore."

The irony is that this lonely man now has the love of a beautiful young Italian countess. This part of the novel is all Hemingway and recounts an actual Hemingway love affair.

Across the River was not well received. Lanham/Hemingway did not work. The book's defects include padded descriptions of the food and drink consumed by the hero and heroine. Lots of talk about food. One critic said the title should have been *Across the Street and Into the Grill.*

But Hemingway was not down for the count. In 1953, *The Old Man and the Sea* won the Pulitzer Prize. This was followed in 1959 by the Nobel Prize for literature. He was described as one of the great American writers who changed the way novels are written, with his simple and direct style combined with emotional power.

Hemingway died in 1961 from a self-inflicted wound. Lanham retired from the army in 1954 and died in 1978. He was buried with honors in Arlington National Cemetery.

THIS &
THAT

WE MEET BY CHANCE

There are strange coincidences in life: they occur so *à propos* that the strongest minds are impressed, and ask if that mysterious and inexorable fatality in which the ancients believed, is not really the law that governs the world.

Alfred Mercier

I practice law near Connecticut Avenue and K Street. The headwaters of Connecticut Avenue consist of two separate tributaries. One tributary bearing the name Connecticut Avenue starts near the White House and trickles northward along the east side of Farragut Square, past the Army and Navy Club and then to K Street. It joins the other tributary that starts somewhere around Constitution Avenue and goes by the name of 17th Street. It moves northward past the Baltimore Orioles shop until it gets to the west side of Farragut Square at K Street. There the tributaries merge and the real Connecticut Avenue commences. It proceeds northward as a grand avenue from K Street to Dupont Circle and from Dupont Circle it moves into Maryland and then continues up the East Coast under various names until it gets lost someplace in Canada.

Farragut Square, the park that separates the tributaries, is a park for locals. The downtown bicycle messengers meet there in the morning and compare earnings and schedules. On good weather days it is a park filled with office workers out for an hour in the sunshine. At noon all the benches are taken. The continuous art deco benches that decorate New York's Central Park would be better than the separate benches and would provide more bench space.

Dupont Circle is a cheerful park to just hang out in and watch what goes on. There is a Washington Square feel to it. People are not in a hurry. There are people who are comfortable being out of work. There are chess players, bicyclists, dog walkers, strollers, and Social Security check experts. Dupont Circle's benches are continuous, providing room for everybody. The center fountain offers a splashing diversion from just watching the people. If further diversion is required, take a walk over to the outside bookstall of Second Story Books. Buy a book for two dollars, take it back to Dupont Circle, and read a few pages to see if you caught a bargain.

Yesterday a policeman on horseback appeared in Dupont Circle. The horse was elegant in all respects and dignified to the point of intimidating the benchers. A mid-day sight of a man on horseback clears the mind of the bytes and macros of computer jargon.

When out for a walk along Connecticut Avenue I carry an expectancy of a meeting by chance with one of a number of especially interesting lawyers I have known whose office is within three or four blocks of my office. But for some strange reason such a chance meeting is rare. When I do have the good luck to meet such a friend we talk of the ups and downs of the law practice. The judges we like and dislike. The peculiarities of clients. How things have changed and who is getting all the good cases. The distinctive element is that we are genuinely pleased to meet. The short conversation is what should take place but never does at a class reunion. There is too much formality at reunions and there are too many people we do not recognize. And there is too much of the need to have something to say despite the fact that years have gone by and we do not know each other anymore. Reunions carry intimations of mortality. The reunion program lists those who have joined the silent majority and those who cannot be traced and those who have chosen to disappear.

Ten years ago my wife and I were walking along London's Bond Street observing the throngs of Londoners who live and die knowing nothing of us just as we live and die knowing nothing of them. All its hustle and bustle unaffected by our presence or absence. I was also reflecting on the presence of the delicate fragrance of fine cigar smoke that is ever-present in London's West End. Londoners pay Dunhill and Davidoff top prices for cigars to provide us nonsmokers the pleasant aroma of a smoldering Cuban wrapper. As we turned off Bond into the Burlington Arcade, whom do we see but Milton Gelenian. Milton's office is at Connecticut and K in Washington, but I never see him. We never meet in our own neighborhood, where we are within a few city blocks of each other. But here we meet by chance in London, three thousand miles away. And here he is, big as life, smoking a big Cuban Perfecto Magnifico and looking like a Londoner. A thousand or more subordinate events clicked into place to bring us together at 2 p.m. London time. We adjourn to the dining room at Brown's

Hotel to evaluate this astonishing turn of events. The conversation is *dee*lightful. We speak of cause and effect, and how the fates laugh at probabilities. We speak of coincidence. Do coincidences suggest there is a larger meaning if only we can discover it? Are they a look behind the prosaic into a fifth dimension?

This brings into the discussion the role the fates play in our lives. How much of what we do is preordained? Are we all involved in a game played against a concealed adversary?

When we complete our Brown's Hotel meeting, Milton walks toward Piccadilly and my wife and I continue our Bond Street stroll under the spell of an occurrence that did not happen except for the fact that it did. Years go by before Milton and I meet again. It happens to be at the bus stop at Connecticut and K.

This afternoon I shall walk up Connecticut Avenue to Dupont Circle with the same expectancy of meeting a friend I seldom see. Over the years the number of people within that circle of expectancy has decreased, a circle that grows smaller and smaller as the years dwindle down to a precious few. I would very much like to see one of them on the walk up to Dupont Circle, and if not on the walk up perhaps chance will work its wonders on the walk back. I have a feeling today will be such a day.

A JUBILEE YEAR

The Bible identifies a jubilee year. It is each fiftieth year of the calendar. It is a year of forgiveness. The jubilee year nullifies commercial obligations that have accumulated over the preceding 49 years. It nullifies mortgages, promissory notes, and extortionate loans. The preceding 49 years' worth of statutory governmental detritus disappears. Gone. Jubilee year is a chance to begin again. Its spirit, with modifications, is to be found in chapters 7 and 11 of the Bankruptcy Act.

Biblical commentators say the jubilee year concept was impractical even in biblical times. Nevertheless the concept is well grounded in wisdom.

The mechanical enactment of regulations by city, state, and federal legislative bodies builds an awesome statutory slag heap. Laws once enacted rarely are repealed. So they stack up higher and higher and interact with each other. Paragraph 2(c) can be understood only by reference to 28 U.S.C. § 1925, as amended—and so on.

From time to time there is an impulse to sort through the accumulation and dispose of the regulations that never should have been and the ones whose time has come and gone. Rarely does something come of such a proposal. The energy and skill required to perform the task are underestimated. A friend who worked on a commission created to reduce government paperwork said that talent for such work is the talent of the anarchist. It resides with people who get great satisfaction by throwing things out in bulk. Such people do not take to committee work. They don't keep a log of what has been trashed because they know in their hearts that the log is just more trash. Therefore the committees fall under the control of those with a retention bias.

I would like to see the biblical jubilee-year concept applied to court rules, the rules enacted by every local court and every local judge. These are the spider webs of the law. These are the razor-sharp coral reefs wounding those who navigate near the courthouse. We need flat tax-type local rules. Rules that cannot be expanded except by a super-majority. Rules that a busy practitioner can keep, in general terms, in the hat.

Judge Robert H. Keeton has this to say concerning rules:

Rules of procedure should facilitate consideration of the merits. Trial and preparation for trial should not become a game of moves in which the judge, as umpire, calls players out for not touching bases, and in the right sequence. (50 Pitt L. Rev. 853)

Given the obvious good sense of Judge Keeton's words, why do local rules creep in everywhere? Tip O'Neill said all politics is local, and so, too, is law practice. It is shaped by the near—the time and the place. And what is special to time and place is entangled by a primitive logic of its own. Courts in the same jurisdiction have used different-size paper. Some courts require that papers be filed with a blue backing. Others forbid a backing, no matter the color. Charlie Chaplin, in *Limelight*, declared life to be the composite of daily dealings with the butcher, the baker, and the candlestick maker and all within walking distance from home. The need to give local color to what we do may have Darwinian survival value. It is tribal. It connects the locals together against the foreigner.

Years ago I attended a meeting of lawyers who had just been named as defendants in a law firm split-up case. The plaintiffs hired a nationally known out-of-town lawyer who neglected to get local counsel. There was a discussion about how the presence of this lawyer would affect the case. It was agreed that our side might win simply because the nationally known out-of-towner would surrender once he tried to figure out our local rules. To get a motion filed in the court where the suit was pending, one had to respond correctly to questions as arcane as those asked in the multistate bar exam concerning the Uniform Commercial Code.

Books could be written on the art of selecting local counsel. In addition to knowing the local rules, published and unpublished, local counsel must know how to get a subpoena served in a hurry. Local counsel must be loyal. In small communities, long-standing loyalties may override loyalties of the moment.

I have had interesting experiences with local counsel in rural jurisdictions where local counsel may spell the difference between winning and losing. I've worked with locals whose family members practiced law in the community for three generations. They can eyeball a jury as the case progresses and tell me when to hold and when to fold.

I like local counsel whose office is close by the courthouse. This is an advantage when papers must be prepared on short notice. And the office is a place to hang out during the inevitable delays in trial work. It is a place to eat during the luncheon recess. The food served in the lunchrooms of nearby small-town courthouses gives cause for apprehension.

One day I hope to receive an invitation to an ecumenical jubilee local-rules conference when all local rules will be abolished and we start all over again. And just as the present rules limit interrogatories to 30, including subparts, so will the new rules be capped at 30, including subrules.

At the committee meetings I would question the rule that requires counsel to allege in every motion that counsel met to discuss whether the motion was to be conceded. I know of no case where opposing counsel conceded a motion for summary judgment or a motion to dismiss. I question the value of such meetings even in discovery motions. Perhaps a better rule would require counsel's filing a discovery motion to assert that counsel met and in a spirit of utmost candor discussed personal problems of common concern such as difficult partners, family problems, the ingratitude and greed of clients, the unpredictability of judges. Such a discussion might well bring about agreement on many things, including better answers to plaintiff's interrogatory 25.

ARRESTED IN
OLD HAVANA

T he other day I saw in the window of an antique shop a huge leather-bound record book. It must have weighed 50 pounds. The hand-tooled binding displayed the scales of justice. I recalled seeing such a book when I was in Havana, Cuba, in the 1950's. I was told then that contracts in Cuba were unenforceable unless written out in a formal record book, signed by the parties, and sworn to before the recording officer. Oral agreements were unenforceable. Whether that is an accurate statement of the Cuban law, I do not know, but it certainly is the way to eliminate a substantial amount of litigation.

The antique book also brought to mind a significant event that occurred during my brief Havana trip. In the pre-Castro days, Havana advertised itself as the Paris of the Caribbean. Those in search of Cuban rum and corona cigars—the authentic Monte Cristos, the Cohibas, the Simon Bolivars—strolled up and down Havana's broad avenues. Two friends and I took that stroll and found our way into a Cuban rum factory, samples given on the premises. One of my friends drank too many samples and he got into a fight with a cabdriver.

Police were called. They arrested the three of us. We were walked over to the central Havana police station. The police took a long statement from each of us, converted it into Spanish, and entered it in a huge hand-tooled leather-bound record book. Each page was lined and numbered. I was impressed that all proceedings were duly recorded in the book of record. There was formality to the proceedings. We were in a court of record. We had the protections of due process.

I was invited to write in the book my version of what happened. I wrote out a few sentences. Then, overcome with the futility of it, I decided to trust to luck and the hope that *deus ex machina* would intervene.

We took seats in chairs lined up against the wall. We remained there for an hour or so. I noticed that, as people were brought in, the facts were carefully entered in the record book.

The chief of police was seated behind a large desk. In his uniform he looked like an overweight leader of a Shriners marching band. He took telephone calls. He consulted with clerks. He adjudicated cases. He turned some arrestees loose. He detained others. And he did it all while listening to a baseball game on the radio.

In time the chief called on us to declare what happened. After listening to our confused presentation, he requested a statement from the arresting officer, who spoke in Spanish. Then he directed the cabdriver to testify. His presentation became quite emotional. Thereafter we were told that our case was much too complicated for summary adjudication. The formal hearing was set for two weeks later. What were we to do until the case was to be heard?

I, being a lawyer, was directed by my two friends to speak. I asked the chief whether there was a bondsman in attendance. A bondsman stepped forward. He advised the chief that we needed a short recess. Motion granted.

The bondsman said he had heard the testimony. We were in great danger. The chief was temperamental. He may not grant bond. He may detain us until the case was to be heard, two weeks hence.

As this was being said, the chief of police coughed. He coughed again. He announced he must have *agua*. He shouted, "*agua, agua*." He coughed again. In response to the *agua* command, a police officer hurried over to the impressive leather-bound record book. He ripped out several pages and folded them into paper cups to be filled with water from a nearby spigot. That astonishing disrespect for the official record of proceedings remains in my mind to this day.

Then our bondsman took charge. He asked who was the treasurer of our group. Our treasurer was the one with ready cash. He stepped forward. The bondsman, who asked to be called Felix, told us we must cool off the complainant, the cabdriver. Felix said he would arrange for the cabby to drive us to the airport. It will be the usual fare plus a substantial getaway bonus. Felix spoke to the cabdriver. The deal was made. Then Felix approached the chief of police. They whispered together. The cabby was called forward to join in the whispering.

Felix had the qualities that define a great advocate. His happiness was to have a new client and to prove to that client that he, Felix, was determined to rearrange reality in accordance with the client's wishes. Fate had determined that this man of considerable lawyerly skills must waste them propitiating a Havana policeman and helping naive tourists jump bond.

The chief then announced that he was inclined to grant bond. He directed the bondsman to post the $150 for each of us as a guarantee that we would appear for trial. The chief warned us that failing to appear for trial was a very serious offense. Did I see the chief wink at Felix? I thought I did.

We settled accounts with Felix. He ordered the cabdriver to take us nonstop to the airport.

Before we made our getaway I had an impulse to do something audacious. I asked if I could have a drink of water. Felix went over to that beautiful leather-bound log book of record. He ripped out several pages. He made paper cups. He filled them with water and passed them around. I could see on the pages of my cup the graceful penmanship (slightly blurred by the water) of the recording officer's official report, which, under the federal rules of Cuban evidence, would be entitled to the presumption of regularity and authenticity.

CONGRESSIONAL HEARINGS, PARDONS, AND FALL GUYS

When I was much younger and much wiser than I am now, I occasionally found myself at a strategy meeting among older lawyers. These older lawyers were cautious in expressing their views concerning the correct strategy to solve the client's problems. Their comments were hedged with reservations and contingencies, the need for more facts, and a fear of burning bridges.

Although I knew it was best to say little in such elevated company, I could not keep my mouth shut. I spoke up and announced what must be done to protect our client. Then one of the group would say, "It's a good idea and you should go with it." Notice the change in the pronoun from "we" to "you." Being young and enthusiastic, I did not notice that switch.

The person who has the self-evident solution to a complicated problem must ask: Why am I the only brilliant person in the room? Why hasn't somebody else, not me, claimed credit for this perfect solution? The answer is that a complicated problem is a game of pickup sticks. One stick cannot be moved without producing a new arrangement of the sticks requiring a new strategy for extracting the next stick.

On reflection, my idea on such occasions was not so good after all. In fact, it was a bad idea. In addition, it would bring embarrassment to the person connected with it. With the passage of time came the realization that I had been backed into the role of the fall guy.

Now when I am in a conference room and a young and energetic lawyer speaks up with the perfect solution, I have the common decency to tell him that the idea has already been considered and rejected. Rejected because there may be subtle ethical issues involved. Rejected because the judge in the case would not look favorably upon such an approach. Rejected because it may bring on problems much greater than the ones we now confront.

Watergate used up a whole cadre of young ambitious lawyers who offered the perfect solution to the President's problems. These young, ambitious lawyers discovered that their leader had withheld information from them and furthermore they themselves closed their eyes to the dangers involved. They were the fall guys. Even an experienced person, such as John N. Mitchell, the former attorney general and Nixon campaign manager, was made a fall guy.

Wouldn't it be interesting if we had a transcript of an Oval Office conversation when President Nixon was setting up his fall guys? As a matter of fact we have such a transcript.

On May 8, 1973, at 12:43 p.m., a friend of President Nixon's, Donald Kendall, enters the Oval Office and explains how Nixon can make his closest associates, Bob Haldeman and John Ehrlichman, the fall guys. Kendall says to Nixon: "The only thing people believe is a leak." Therefore Nixon must create a leak. He must write a memorandum to Chief of Staff Alexander Haig and in the memorandum "you want to blister Haldeman and Ehrlichman and this, I know, it is a tough thing for you to do." Nixon had publicly defended Haldeman and Ehrlichman, and people admired him for that. But now Nixon must think of himself.

> Kendall: You give me the memorandum. I will guarantee that Jack Anderson will print it. … in other words you go through all the problems that you've had the last few months and what it meant to you to do it with Haldeman and Ehrlichman and then you have to blister them and say that they let you down by not keeping you informed and that you don't want something like this to happen without being informed of all the details because this attacks the integrity of the office.

> Nixon: I think it's a very good idea. I'll write something.

How many fall guys did you count? I count two and maybe three.

As we watch the current pardon hearings, we shall see some good and honorable people discover that they had been converted into fall guys.

There was a song of yesteryear that puts it all in rhyme. The great Bert Williams talked and sang the words that follow, in *The Ziegfeld Follies of 1919*. The accompanying music to the song is slow and mournful, with reliance on oboe solos in the minor chords.

> *Now the circus played our town one day*
> *And three Bengal tigers got away.*
> *The manager in charge came up to me and said—*
> *My friend, here's your opportunity.*

Somebody's got to go and get them cats—
Because the tiger man is sick in bed, so he said.
The man who catches them alive
A real hero he's going to be.

I said, yes sir. A wonderful chance for somebody, I do agree.
A wonderful opportunity for somebody else, not me.

Cubes with ebony dots
Often lead to cemetery lots.
For instance last night brought on a fight
Which finished up with fists and shots.
I was the furthest from the door.
The others all got there before.
A body on the floor lay dead.
And through the transom someone said—
Somebody's got to stay behind—
Somebody must remain—
So when the officers arrive—
That somebody will explain
Why our dear brother here ain't alive.

Yes, it's a wonderful chance for somebody, I do agree.
Yes, a wonderful opportunity for somebody else, not me.

So the next time you see a wonderful opportunity to be a
hero, just hum to yourself, *Yes, a wonderful opportunity for somebody—somebody else, not me.*

DAUMIER IN
MOTIONS COURT

What you would see in a French court of law would bear a significant resemblance to what you would see in a court in London, New York, Berlin, or Hong Kong. You would see lawyers, litigants, witnesses, and clerks. In most courts the lawyers wear black robes and the litigants wear the look of apprehension. Nothing good is going to happen. In Honoré Daumier's drawings now on display at the Phillips Collection, the lawyers not only wear black robes, they wear black hats. The costume of the advocate inhibits the judge from falling into the habit of treating the wrongdoing of the client as the wrongdoing of the lawyer.

Daumier demonstrates his comprehensive knowledge of the judicial process by the way he catches the posture typical of a lawyer telling a witness exactly what to say. And there are drawings depicting a lawyer telling the witness that what he has just said was fatal to his claim. The case is lost. All that preparation gone like a snowflake on the water.

Daumier transmits the atmosphere of delay that hangs heavily over all judicial proceedings. Too many things must work in unison for a judicial proceeding to start on time. Going to court is a waiting game. It always has been and always will be from the beginning of time to the end of time.

Daumier particularly enjoyed laying on the line of the grease crayon showing the lawyer pleading the client's cause, leaning forward with arms outstretched, engaged in a bathetic yearning for simple justice for his client who sits close by in awe of his lawyer's performance. A moment ago the advocate was half asleep. Now the curtain is up, and he is an operatic performer.

In several of Daumier's drawings I see what must have been a French motions court in the 1850's. All motions courts are alike. The motions clerk notifies the lawyers to appear at ten o'clock for the motions calendar. Everybody responds and the vigil commences. The law of probabilities states that the lawyer attending a motions calendar at 10 will not be heard before 11:30. A few will even be told that their cases cannot be reached before the luncheon recess and they must return at 1:30. The judge may not take the bench until 11:30. He will apologize. He will say he had important matters in his chambers, important matters that must be attended to. The cynical lawyers have heard this before. They imagine the judge sitting back in his big chair, dipping the tip of the Danish pastry in the caffe latte.

Once the judge settles in, the clerk asks for preliminary matters. Lawyers move forward to address the court. There will be a few announcements that the motion has been resolved. The judge compliments the lawyers on their maturity in reaching agreement.

Next will be the requests for continuances of the hearing on the motion. Here the true resourcefulness of counsel is on display.

The file was lost. He never got the notice until yesterday. Discovery is not complete. The motion was prepared and was to be argued by co-counsel who is engaged in a trial in another court. The judge is unsympathetic. He is a student of *Williston on Continuances*, the authoritative text. He insists that the motion be withdrawn without prejudice, otherwise he will dismiss it with prejudice. The judge always wins. And now the clerk's first reading of this morning's calendar. Please announce "ready" when your motion is called.

What should one do between 10 and the time one's motion is to be heard? It is a time to read. The best reading matter for motions court consists of books that are soothing, passive, meditative, books that generally woo the imagination, sedative books, calming the mind and so composing the body and spirit that one can rise when his name is called, showing no irritation at having arrived at 10 to speak at 12.

The books I have in mind are rambling and discursive, neither too boring nor too exciting, interesting on every page but dramatic nowhere, with a stream of events but no definite break— the kind that can be put down so that one can give attention to the embarrassment of a fellow lawyer, at the hands of a short-tempered judge, and picked up again after this pleasant interlude, without the feeling that one has lost the thread.

It is also helpful if the book is elevated and urbane in tone so that one's legal argument, when given, will benefit from recent exposure to elegant prose.

Spirited literature is dangerous. If you were reading about the French Revolution, for instance, you might indulge a rebellious urge to say to the judge upon being told that your case will be carried over to 1:30, "Then why was I called here at 10 when a little foresight would have made it self-evident that six applications for temporary restraining orders, and four motions for summary judgment, could not all be disposed of at 10?"

There is no end to the amount of information you can gather from books while awaiting contingencies like the motions calendar. Lord Chesterfield, in his letters to his son, mentions a man who was able to read the entire *Greek Anthology* and most of the Latin classics in the few minutes he took each day responding to the calls of nature.

The sight of a courtroom filled with lawyers, all with books of a different size, shape, and color in front of them, could provoke a judge to enjoin the practice of reading in the courtroom.

Perhaps this accounts for the publication many years ago of nonlegal books bound in sheepskin to look like law books. Now and then, these odd volumes are to be seen at auction sales. I have picked up a few. I have had the pleasure of sitting with such a book in the front row of motions court in sight of a judge who is a stickler for courtroom decorum. The back of the book gave the impression I was reading from an old United States report, when in fact I was enjoying Balzac's *Droll Stories*, occasionally disturbed by the judge's continued repetition of the words, "Don't you know I can't grant a summary judgment if there is a question of fact?"

If the judge could have seen through the cover of my book, he would have exclaimed:

> *Was ever book containing such vile matter*
> *So fairly bound? O, that deceit should dwell*
> *In such a gorgeous place!*

FIGHTING THE BLUES
WITH THE FINE ARTS

To go to court is to court disappointment. A lawyer who never lost a case has tried few cases. There are disappointments even when the case isn't tried to verdict. There is motions court—the long and the short. If going to court is part of your practice, you must find a place to fight the blues that accompany the inevitable disappointments inherent in the adversary system. If your practice is here in Washington, you are in luck. Both the local and the federal courts are close by the National Gallery of Art and the National Portrait Gallery.

The National Gallery of Art is just south of the United States District Court. If you have been dealt an adverse ruling by a judge who does not understand the law of summary judgment, I suggest when you leave the courthouse you stroll down to the National Gallery and refresh yourself surrounded by priceless works of art. Enter the main building, walk up to the second floor and turn left and wander around among the Impressionists. There is something a lawyer can learn from Monet's and Pissarro's Paris street scenes. Up close they are an incomprehensible clutter of colored dots and dashes. Stand back a few feet and they transform into a clearly recognizable busy street. One might say that hundreds of facts, relevant and not so relevant, are converted by the artist into a winning picture that one takes in at a glance. The art of the advocate.

Subtlety is also part of the advocate's art. Things are never black and white. It is the shades of gray that make the difference. Take a look at Manet's "Death of a Toreador." As I recall the picture, Manet sparingly used the blacks and whites to outline the body of the toreador and a dot of red to show the toreador's bleeding wound. In between are the twenty shades of grey that show the skill of the artist.

If the case you lose was tried in the local Superior Court, you leave the court and walk north to Eighth and F streets. There you find the National Portrait Gallery. Within it is inspiration. You will see a stirring portrait of Theodore Roosevelt, caught by the artist in the act of reciting these stirring words:

> Far better it is to dare mighty things, to win glorious triumphs, even though checkered by failure, than to take rank with those poor spirits who neither enjoy much nor suffer much, because they live in the gray twilight that knows not victory nor defeat.

Both the National Portrait Gallery and the National Gallery of Art have interior courtyards where one sits alone and meditates and considers life's big questions such as, Why didn't I take another deposition? Why did I assume that the judge had read the papers?

Winston Churchill, in his book *Painting as a Pastime*, says there are many remedies for life's disappointments. He identifies exercise, travel, play, and other diversions. He then says that what is common to all these is the need to change course when things go bad. He discovered that the best change for him was painting. "Happy are the painters, for they shall not be lonely. Light and color, peace and hope, will keep them company to the end, or almost to the end, of the day." When Churchill was in his state of depression during the lonely 1930's, an artist friend told him to buy a paint box, paints, and some big brushes. Churchill was told that the quality that was needed to get started was not years devoted to the study of drawing, perspective, and the science of color. He was too old for that. All he needed was what he had, courage and audacity. Get big splashes of paint on a canvas and the sooner the better. He started up and discovered that big brushes and lots of paint bring good luck on a canvas. He discovered what everyone who paints discovers. Within the splashes and smears one sees well-drawn landscapes and portraits.

Churchill's studio is preserved at Chartwell, his estate outside London. It is worth a trip to Chartwell just to see Churchill's painting setup. The studio is in a little brick house away from the main house. Visitors are told it is maintained just as it was when Churchill used it. As one can see, he used big brushes and lots of paint.

Churchill had advantages that most amateurs do not have. He had friends who were skilled painters, and when he encountered a problem beyond his competence he had an artist friend look over his shoulder and give him some advice.

There is a photograph in the Chartwell main house of Churchill at lunch with his professional artist friends. One of the artists is Walter Sickert, whose influence can be detected in Churchill's landscapes. In addition to landscapes, Sickert liked to paint the interiors of music halls and the second-rate music hall performers. A few years ago I came across a book of Sickert's paintings. It looked to me, in my own spirit of audacity, that Sickert's painting called "That Wonderful Mother of Mine" would be easy to copy. It is a picture of a music hall singer all dressed up in white tie and tails, standing at the footlights singing a sentimental ballad in memory of his wonderful mother. Audacity carried me forward, and the picture turned out to be worth my investing in a moderately expensive frame.

The effort to copy the painting of a skilled artist, just making that effort, teaches more about the art and the appreciation of painting than hours of abstract lectures. I commend it to you. It makes no difference that you have no talent. In fact, the absence of talent gives you an insight into the complicated sleight of hand required of the professional artist. Better off doing some work with the oils and brushes than standing in line for a van Gogh exhibit.

IN A LITTLE TIN BOX

I drop into bookstores on the way home to look over the stock to see what is new. The other evening while taking a look around in Chapters, the bookstore at 15th and K streets heavy into literature, I took down a copy of Robert Frost's collected poetry. In flipping the pages I found this:

Never ask of money spent
Where the spender thinks it went.
Nobody was ever meant
To remember or invent
What he did with every cent.

Robert Frost entitled that bit of verse "The Hardships of Accounting." I have a better title: "The White-Collar Crime Defense."

When the government decides to close in on somebody who spends but has no legitimate source of income, the government does want to know about every cent. The respondent responds by saying nobody was ever meant, etc., etc. The government may meet the resort to poetry with the net-worth theory. *Holland v. United States*, 348 U.S. 121 (1954).

The net-worth theory confronts Frost's principle by proving evasion of federal income taxes and other things by circumstantial evidence, showing that the taxpayer's wealth is greater than reflected in his income tax returns. The disparity is unreported taxable income.

The federal government's use of evidentiary techniques of this kind has been common over a relatively long period of time. In a typical net-worth prosecution the government, having concluded that the taxpayer's records are inadequate as a basis for determining income, attempts to establish an opening net worth, that is, the total net value of the taxpayer's assets at the beginning of a given year. The government then proves increases in the taxpayer's net worth for each succeeding year during the period under examination and calculates the difference. The taxpayer's nondeductible expenditures, including living expenses, are added to these increases. When the resulting figure for any year is substantially greater than the taxable income reported, the government has the audacity to claim that the excess is unreported taxable income.

How does one explain unexplainable increases in wealth? How does one explain large cash expenditures from funds that never entered a bank account?

In 1930 Samuel Seabury was appointed by Governor Franklin D. Roosevelt to investigate corruption in the administration of Mayor James J. Walker of New York City. The investigation triggered explanations that test the imaginative possibilities of

those asked to make an accounting. A number of vice squad officers accumulated tens of thousands of dollars in their bank
accounts. How come? asked Seabury.

One vice squad officer, James Quinlivan, was asked to
explain the $31,000 that suddenly appeared in his bank account.
Quinlivan said he won $10,000 of it 20 years earlier, on a horse
called Flora Belle. He got $10,000 cash when his father died. He
kept all this in a trunk in his house. Later, on his honeymoon, he
won $3,000 more at the races, bringing his cash reserve up to
$23,000. The remaining $8,000 he won at cards.

Robert E. Morris, another member of the vice squad,
needed to account for $50,000. He said $10,000 came from gambling (before he joined the force, of course), and the remaining
$40,000 was given to him twenty-one years earlier by Uncle
George, now dead. He happened to bump into George at Coney
Island. Uncle George peeled forty brand-new one-thousand-
dollar bills off his roll and handed them to his beloved nephew.

> Q: Why would Uncle George, with a wife and three chil-
> dren of his own, be so generous?
>
> A: I was always his favorite nephew, he always thought a lot
> of me.

Seabury next turned his attention to Sheriff Farley, who was
asked to shed some light on how, during the past seven years, he
managed to bank $396,000 when his seven years of wages totaled
only $87,000. After Farley gave his answers he became famous as
"Tin-Box" Farley.

> Q: Will you tell the Committee where you could have got-
> ten that sum of money?
>
> A: Monies that I had saved.

Q: Where did you keep these monies that you had saved?

A: In a big box in a big safe.

Q: Was [it] fairly full when you withdrew the money?

A: It was full.

Q: Was this big box that was safely kept in the big safe a tin box?

A: A tin box.

Q: What is the most money you ever put in that tin box you have?

A: I had as much as $100,000 in it.

Q: When did you deposit that?

A: From time to time.

In a like manner, Seabury questioned Farley about his bank deposits in 1927, 1928, and 1929, always receiving the same reply, that the cash to make the deposits came from the tin box. Coming to 1930, the committee counsel noted that Farley's total deposits had been $65,890 while his salary had been $12,876. How could Farley account for the discrepancy?

"Well, that came from the good box I had," said Farley. Laughter filled the hearing room.

"Kind of a magic box?" asked Seabury.

"It was a wonderful box," replied the sheriff.

Frost was right. Nobody was ever meant to remember or invent.

INTERROGATION

"Self-determination" one of them insisted.

"Arbitration" cried another.

"Co-operation?" suggested the mildest of the party.

"Confiscation!" answered an uncompromising female.

I, too, became slightly intoxicated by the sound of these vocables. And were they not the cure for all our ills?

"Inebriation!" I chimed in, "Inundation, Afforestation, Flagellation, Transubstantiation, Co-Education!"

Logan Pearsall Smith

This mood of gathering excitement and rising declamation overtakes me as I warm up to the dictation of interrogatories. Once past the preliminaries such as name, address, and occupation, I then go for my adversary's protected area. As I conjure up questions of unbelievable ingenuity, I can hardly contain myself. When I develop the question which I know will paralyze my opponent, I suspend the work and take a walk around the room.

My enthusiasm is fueled by righteous indignation at the very fact that the defendant had the presumption to file an answer to my well drawn complaint. How dare he deny what I so beautifully alleged in numbered paragraphs! Once I complete the final draft of the interrogatories, my confidence in the outcome of the case is at its highest pitch. These cunning questions are unanswerable. We will never settle this case. We have momentum. The rascals are on the run.

All of this changes after the expiration of thirty days when the answers come in. Most of my questions are disposed of with a "see above," or an "irrelevant," or "attorney work product." The penetrating interrogatory concerning experts' reports is deftly handled with a "no experts have submitted *written* reports."

As I read the evasive answers my indignation returns. Who does he think he is? I will file a Motion to Compel together with a Rule 37 motion requesting costs and attorneys fees. But before these motions are dictated, I must deal with the interrogatories that now have been sent to me. When I examine them, I see right away that my opponent has turned all the questions around and dictated them back to me. In addition, he has added twenty-four more questions (not including subparts). The very thought of spending a day or two with that crazy client of mine to frame answers gives me the chills. He will come in with all those scraps of paper and those documents out of chronological order. He'll cover my desk with them. We'll never get through. Then there will be the problem of trying to collect from him the bill for photocopying it all.

What I better do is file this motion to compel with the motion for costs and attorneys fees and see what that does. But if I do that, my opponent may turn those motions against me when he gets our evasive answers.

"Hello, Frank? I would like to talk to you about the Simp-son case—you know, the case with all the interrogatories? Let's stop wasting time. I have authority to accept in full settlement—now this is a rock-bottom figure. ... "

KEEP YOUR
BIG MOUTH SHUT

Many years ago, I brought a client to the office of Charlie Ford, then one of Washington's leading criminal lawyers. As Charlie droned on to the alleged wrongdoer a mechanical warning about the dangers of discussing the case with anyone, absolutely anyone, my eyes wandered around the office.

It was not an orderly place to conduct business. Here and there were small calendars of years gone by bearing the insignia of bail bondsmen. In a dusty corner, yellowed and outdated pocket-parts for *Corpus Juris Firstum* or *Secundum* teetered, one on the other. Old file folders filled the nooks and crannies. On one wall were pictures of distinguished and obviously influential people who, judging by their attire, died before I was born. There was one unique artifact that caught my eye—a large mounted fish on a back wall. Beneath it were these words: *If I Had Kept My Big Mouth Shut, I Wouldn't Be Here.*

Sometime later I asked Charlie to give me the history of the mounted fish. He said it was a gift from a part-time criminal who had a superb instinct for self-preservation and who liked to repeat that there are no deaf and dumb people in jail.

If you were to drop by my office today, you would see that I have my own fish. Every now and then an alleged defendant, as he sits in my office narrating his troubles, lets his gaze wander over to the fish on the wall and the telling inscription beneath it. He is thinking if he had kept his big mouth shut, he wouldn't be paying lawyers.

As a young lawyer watching my elders perform, I was duly impressed with lawyers like Charlie Ford. Charlie, despite his fish's admonition of silence, was a table pounder and a screamer. When he made his closing arguments, his voice rang throughout the courthouse. This was a natural reflection of his personality. He was a buoyant, self-confident man. Charlie loved to talk, and the talk overflowed throughout the courtroom. On reflection, his advocacy assayed out at 20 percent high-grade bombast, 50 percent persuasive argument, and the remainder the customary legal platitudes. He had many imitators, myself included.

Lloyd Paul Stryker, the renowned New York trial lawyer whose book *The Art of Advocacy* is still worth reading, was another great talker and screamer. I made a trip to New York in the late 1940's to see him perform. Stryker was not just a screamer. He was a vigorous denouncer of evil wherever it had the presumption to appear against his client of the moment. If Stryker made an occasional mistake in cross-examination, he just continued on and talked his way out of it or examined so long that nobody could recall it. His last bravura performance was in defense of Alger Hiss at Hiss's first trial, which ended in a hung jury.

In time I gave up the idea of becoming a screamer. Among other disabilities, I did not have the required energy. I sought an alternative based on the principle that less is more.

I discovered my role model in the career of an active trial lawyer who was already elderly when I first met him. He continued a full trial practice with a remarkable record of successes until shortly before his death at 86. It was all the more remarkable because he spoke in a voice so soft he could hardly be heard. It was said that you had to hug him to hear him. Not only was he soft of voice—he said little. No extra words.

The innate character of some people serves them best in either youth or maturity; at one of those times, the character and the age complement each other. This was true of my role model. His natural talent for circumspect silence perfectly matched his mature years.

His career was well over before the Federal Rules of Evidence were adopted, but he anticipated Rule 403, which states that evidence may be excluded if it is a waste of time or is the needless presentation of cumulative evidence. In accordance with that rule, he wasted no time, and he rarely presented needless cumulative evidence. It is an approach that takes courage. The impulse is to put on every witness who can help. He did not do that. He believed one good witness is enough. Cumulative witnesses may end up impeaching the single good one.

The concept of brevity found in Rule 403 reflects the words of the Tao, the ancient Chinese philosophical work that teaches the eloquence of silence and the virtue of simplicity. It is filled with such raisins of mystical wisdom as "He who knows does not speak and he who speaks does not know." A commentator described it as the first enunciated philosophy of camouflage in the world.

My education in the rewards of keeping my mouth shut has been gradual. Of course, I am still learning. Several lessons stand out.

Some years ago, I was to appear before a federal judge in a foreign jurisdiction. I called a friend, who knew the venue, to take counsel on local custom. I was told that, in the words of my informant, "The judge likes to chew on whoever is at the lectern." My friend reinforced the advice with this anecdote: He and his brother (now a federal judge) were representing a defendant in a hopeless criminal case before the jurist in question. When the government rested, my friend told his brother to stand up and move for judgment of acquittal. The brother asked, "What is the basis for the motion?" The reply was, "There is no basis but do it anyway. And sit down right away." The motion was duly made. The prosecutor grabbed the lectern and started up with a long reply. When the judge's catechism of the prosecutor was over, three counts of the indictment were out of the case. The rule of decision seemed to be whoever talks most loses.

When my turn came to speak before this judge, I said, following instructions, I submitted on the papers but I had no objection to my opponent's addressing the court. Well, my opponent did address the court—and then the chewing began. The judge found fault with every fact and principle of law my opponent mentioned.

I have learned that there are judges who turn against whatever is said, as kites rise against the wind. A presentation may commence as a winner in the first five minutes, grow doubtful in the next five minutes, and then untangle completely because the judge comes up with a question counsel did not expect and cannot answer.

Joseph Welch, chief counsel for the Army in the 1954 McCarthy hearings, said that those hearings were where "I gained stature as a public figure by keeping still." The tapes show that Joseph Welch said nothing until he had just the right moment to speak. His silence provided the frame for the attack on Sen. Joseph McCarthy that contributed to McCarthy's downfall. On the other hand, McCarthy could not keep his mouth shut. McCarthy's comment that gave Welch his opening was an unnecessary interruption. To say the right thing at the right time, a lawyer must keep still most of the time.

There are several apocryphal stories about the one question too many on cross-examination. First is the defendant's lawyer who asked the witness whether he saw the defendant bite off the plaintiff's ear. The witness said he didn't. Then this:

Lawyer (proudly): Then tell us how you know my client
bit off the plaintiff's ear.
Witness: I saw your client spit it out.

In another such story, the defense lawyer wishes to establish that the plaintiff did not complain of injuries at the scene of the train wreck and therefore his present complaints are contrived:

Defense lawyer: You now claim you were injured in
the train wreck?
Plaintiff: Yes.
Defense lawyer: Did you complain at the scene?
Plaintiff: No.
Defense lawyer (again, proudly): You didn't complain
because you were not hurt, isn't that so?
Plaintiff: No. I didn't complain because the wreck
caused a horse to break its leg. A man took out a gun
and shot the horse. He then turned towards me and
said "Anyone else around here who got hurt?"

I was told of a criminal case in which an extensive cross-examination resulted in a conviction. When the judge asked the defendant if he had anything to say before the imposition of sentence, the defendant replied, "Yes, Your Honor, in sentencing me, please take into consideration the incompetence of my lawyer."

If I have persuaded you that less may be more, and you wish to experiment with a strategy of silence, you will find that the world suddenly looks different. Instead of a lawyer looking for a chance to speak, you will be a lawyer in search of opportunities to remain silent.

Opportunities to say little occur in appellate practice. In his excellent work *Briefing and Arguing Federal Appeals*, Fritz Wiener has this to say:

> It may be, of course, that the appellant's case is so completely devoid of merit that you, representing the appellee, will never be called upon or that you will be told by the presiding Judge, as you move toward the lectern, "the Court does not desire to hear further argument." In that event, it is better to accept victory gracefully than to attempt to inflict your eloquence on the tribunal. And there may be instances where it will be desirable, on behalf of the appellee, to say little or nothing.
>
> For example, in one case petitioner's lawyer took such a battering from the court that it was obvious to everyone that the judgment below would be affirmed. Counsel for the respondent [Fritz tells me it was Paul Freund] arose, bowed, and said "If the Court please, I must apologize for an error in our brief. At page 39, second line from the bottom, the citation should be to 143 Federal Second and not to 143 Federal." He

paused until the members of the court noted the cor-
rection, paused again when they looked up, toyed with
his watch chain, and proceeded: "Unless there are any
questions, I will submit the respondent's case on the
brief"—and sat down. I have it on excellent authority
that it was one of the most effective arguments ever
heard by that court.

You will find that a good lawyer says nothing when he has
nothing to say. A mature lawyer can watch his opponent make a
mistake and still remain silent. You will not be one of those who
will hear a judge say to you: "Counsel, I've just ruled in your favor.
If you keep on talking, you may convince me to change my mind."

Despite your best intentions, there will be occasions when
logorrhea threatens. You must say something, but you know you
shouldn't. You have something that *must* be heard. Lord Chesterfield in his letters to his son warns against thinking that because
something interests you it will interest others. He tells of a bore
who, whenever there was a lapse in the conversation, would yell,
"What was that? Did you hear that gunshot?" followed by, "Now
that we are talking about guns ..." and off he goes about his obsession, his gun collection.

When we think about it, much of our own lawyer-talk follows the same pattern. We are obsessed with our cases and our
clients. It is painful to let pass an opportunity to describe a clever
turn of events that our skill triggered. Let it go. Nobody in the
game is interested in the victories of a competitor. If you wish to
engage interest, speak of a great loss, a case where you turned
down a million and there was a defendant's verdict. That gets
attention from brethren at the bar. The rest of the blather—con-

trived to set up the autobiographer as a prince of the forum—is best left unsaid.

I can provide the names of two people who might inspire you to keep your mouth shut when there is a compulsion to speak. Each, in his own way, made a substantial contribution to human progress.

First there is Alexander Fleming, one of the discoverers of penicillin. Fleming's biographer said that Fleming responded with vast reservoirs of silence to all questions that conveyed flattery or sought personal information.

Then there is Mahatma Gandhi. He started his career as a working lawyer, trying to get cases and trying to win them. He left the legal profession, not to go into real estate and shopping center development but to pursue other interests. He did community service even though it was not part of a plea bargain requiring Gandhi to plead guilty to one count of price-fixing. Gandhi's biographers tell us he obeyed a self-imposed one-day-a-week of silence. Nothing could make him talk during his silent day—not even the possibility of picking up a good corporate client.

LISTS

I was taking a cab to LaGuardia Airport hoping to catch the two o'clock shuttle back to Washington. As the cabdriver neared the Argosy Bookstore on East 59th Street, I felt a pull I could not resist. I told the cabby to stop. How could I leave New York without looking over the stock in the outside stalls at the Argosy?

The book I bought that day is *Minority Report*, the autobiography of Elmer Rice (1892–1967). I knew of Elmer Rice's interesting career. He started out as a New York City lawyer and became a successful playwright and novelist.

In the book, Mr. Rice records his observations on a jury trial he watched many years ago. He says he was interested more in the performance of one of the well-known trial lawyers than in the subject matter of the case,

> as one might go to see a star, no matter what play. The analogy is close, for the conduct of a jury trial depends

more on the art of acting than upon the science of the law. Frequently all the legal knowledge a trial lawyer needs is an acquaintance with the rules of evidence, which are fairly simple. The day is won by obfuscation, trickery, and histrionics. I saw some notable performers of the time, among them Francis L. Wellman, who wrote several books on the art of cross-examination, and Dudley Field Malone, a smooth rhetorician, who later appeared in the Scopes evolution trial in Tennessee.

Things have changed since those days. Now a trial lawyer must give nights and days to mastering the documents and the depositions, the requests for admissions and the interrogatories. Once that is done there may be some consideration given to the dramatic. Shortly after Mr. Rice was admitted to the bar, he wrote the hit play that changed his life. It was a courtroom drama entitled *On Trial*.

Mr. Rice ends his autobiography with a list summarizing what he says life had taught him. Here is his list:

It is better to live than to die;

to love than to hate;

to create than to destroy;

to do something than to do nothing;

to be truthful than to lie;

to question than to accept;

to be strong than to be weak;

to hope than to despair;

to venture than to fear,

to be free than to be bound.

I like to read lists because I am a list man. Each morning I make a list. The list begins with the date and day of the week. Then follow numbered items identifying the cases of the moment, with a word or two on what needs to be done. Very often some guiding principle, not unlike those on Elmer Rice's list, finds its way in.

Below the main list I write in three or four items concerning which I detect a mental block that prevents me from doing what must be done. My block items vibrate with apprehensions and fear that if I act something will go wrong. But, as Elmer Rice says, it is better to do something than to do nothing. But there are things to be done that I just cannot do. Therefore I ask someone else to take the assignment, someone unaware that I am stumped. If no one is available, I go to a quiet room and close the door. I make a list of all the reasons I am hesitant. In a few minutes I can get at the source of the ominous vibrations. Often it is a sense that doing nothing is the best course.

There are many ways to do nothing. I write letters that are never sent. The drafting of the letter is a valuable exercise. It drains off bitterness, indignation, and confusion. The drafting requires research. It often requires doing something astonishing, like reading the file.

I find my lists from years ago turning up in books and coat pockets. The cases identified on the old lists are over. I can read each of the items without fear. I know how things turned out. Some won, some lost. All gone. Today's list is another story. Each of the items represents something to be done and great uncertainty and anguish concerning how things will turn out.

Anyone making a list to guide oneself through life must include most of Mr. Rice's list. It represents the concentrated wisdom of the human experience. What would be new would be to discover someone who is able to perform, day in and day out, all that is necessary to attain the inner harmony that compliance with the list will bring. We do not need more wisdom. What we need is a Saint-John's-wort type of herbal tea that, once ingested, makes obedience to the list a physiological necessity.

Let me add something of my own to the wisdom literature: Better to jump out of bed in the morning and jog over to the American University track than to hope that a half hour's perfect repose will bring an insight that explains life's otherwise incomprehensible contradictions.

MULTIPLICITY

In his book *Six Memos for the Next Millennium*, Italo Calvino, the Italian novelist, describes an aspect of the modern novel he calls "multiplicity." He says the contemporary novel employs a method where "the least thing is seen as the center of a network of relationships that the writer cannot restrain himself from following, multiplying the detail so that his descriptions and digressions become infinite. Whatever the starting point, the matter in hand spreads out and out, encompassing ever vaster horizons, and if it were permitted to go on further and further in every direction, it would end by embracing the entire universe."

Calvino's words immediately clarified nebulous thoughts I have been carrying around concerning the litigation process.

I became acquainted with the process in the late forties, when I first went to court. In those days the trial lawyers were practical people, a somewhat roguish bunch who had never heard the word "litigator" and who took neither themselves nor their calling too seriously. It was a matter of faith with them to be kind to those met on the way up because you met them all over again on the way down. They worked their cases with a bundle of key facts and a few documents. The court file didn't amount to much in the way of paper. There were the pleadings, a deposition or two, and that was it. Litigation did not take very long and it was inexpensive.

There was another group of lawyers who saw the law as a branch of jurisprudence, a demanding intellectual pursuit conferring an opportunity to exercise great powers of analysis. They shied away from trial work, which they considered somewhat vulgar. Trial work required spending time with witnesses who were never at home and never on time for a meeting.

Then in the sixties the big law firms discovered there was real money in trial work if properly understood. This drew into the game those who should have pursued solipsistic philosophy, astronomy, or experimental biochemistry. All people untrained to grasp the obvious. Such minds when hooked up to $250 an hour produce trouble. Let me repeat Calvino's words: "Whatever the starting point, the matter in hand spreads out and out, encompassing ever vaster horizons, and if it were permitted to go on further and further in every direction, it would end by embracing the entire universe." There is the trouble.

Lawyers called litigators appeared and found that the rules of discovery encourage the matter in hand to go on further and further in every direction. Each fact discovered, each deposition taken, each expert's opinion rendered requires further exploration. So many facts, so many opinions, so many legal memoranda. So much Lexis, Westlaw, Prodigy, and CD-ROM. A concoction inviting one to select, manipulate, and create in accordance with the wishes of the well-funded client. Those with a gift for bringing about the convergence of infinite relationships, past and future, real or possible, gradually took charge of the game.

The principle of multiplicity is also at work in events such as the Kennedy assassination. Too many lines of inquiry are pursued. Disagreements are created rather than resolved. Too many witnesses who cannot be found are identified. Experts discover ways to disagree on key issues. The information expands so no clear conclusion is possible no matter how obvious the events were at the beginning. The seeker after truth passes it by without suspecting he or she has seen it.

I offer two solutions. First, the law. There is too much of it that has no promise of present likelihood.

Samuel Johnson, known as Dictionary Johnson, liked to talk law with his lawyer friend and biographer James Boswell. Boswell recorded a conversation in which Johnson made the point that, when there were few legal precedents, a lawyer's ability to reason logically was prized, but with the increase in precedents, a lawyer's skill depended less on the ability to reason and more on a talent for finding a controlling precedent.

If true when Johnson said it, circa 1776, what is the situation today? We are asphyxiated by legal precedent. For every decision supporting a legal theory there is a countervailing decision discrediting it. All those five-to-four decisions of the Supreme Court chill the tendency toward warm stability. What can we do about it?

I suggest that a lawyer who wishes to cite a case decided before 1950 must pay a fine of $250. A lawyer who wishes to cite any law-review article must pay a fine of $1,000. It would be a felony to cite a case decided before 1935.

Now the facts. The rule of relevance must be changed. As one commentator said, the rule of relevance is the concession of

the law to the shortness of life. Things must be brought to a conclusion by excluding evidence. Rule 401 of the Federal Rules of
Evidence says, "Relevant evidence means evidence having any
tendency to make the existence of any fact that is of consequence
to the determination of the action more probable or less probable
than it would be without the evidence."

That is much too low a standard, given the enormous
resources of information that surround us. Try this modification:
"Relevant evidence means evidence having some real likelihood of
making the existence of a fact of consequence to a determination
of the action significantly more or significantly less probable than it
would be without the evidence, having in mind the backlog."

Any thoughts?

SPIES ARE BACK AT 800 F STREET

Last week after leaving court I took a walk over to nearby Eighth and F streets. There have been stories in the papers about the new, spectacular Spy Museum that just opened there. F Street between Eighth and Ninth has special memories for me. Zola, the restaurant in the museum, is located at 800 F Street, the address of my father's law office.

Those who visit the restaurant will be unaware of the strange tricks the jocular fates can play. My father's secretary was his sister—my aunt. As she grew older, she, as many do when they get old, became suspicious of what was going on around the office. She was sure someone was spying on her. What would she think if she came back today and saw that not only the office but the whole block was given over to spies and spying?

In another strange way she accounts for the fact that the Georgetown University Law Center is near the Capitol rather than near Fifth and E, where it was for many years in those old red-brick buildings. When the university decided to build a new law school close to where the old law school was, situated by the courts, it acquired the property needed except for the one dwelling that would complete the assembly. That one dwelling was owned by my aunt.

One day Milton Kronheim, Sr., called me. As an aside, let me tell you something about Mr. Kronheim. His business was the Kronheim Wholesale Liquor Distributorship. More importantly, he was a sportsman, a good citizen, a philanthropist, and a friend of politicians, including President Harry Truman. It so happened that he and my father went to grade school together.

Now back to the phone call. He said to me, "Jacob, you know there's nothing, absolutely nothing, that I wouldn't do to help Georgetown University. They tell me that your aunt is holding up the construction of the new Georgetown Law School. She will not talk to the Georgetown people who want to buy the property. She will not sell at any price. Jacob, what I must have you do is to get in touch with your aunt and make her listen to reason. I want to do this for Georgetown."

I said to him, "Mr. Kronheim, you are divorced. You know my aunt never married. What you ought to do as a first step is go over to the house and propose to her. That's what you ought to do for Georgetown."

There was a long silence on the phone. When Mr. Kronheim regained his voice, he said, "Jacob, let's say there's *almost* nothing I wouldn't do for Georgetown. "

In the 1930's, Ninth Street between F and Pennsylvania Avenue was filled with people and places of great interest to young men cutting school. It was Washington's tenderloin. On the east side of Ninth Street was the Gayety Burlesk. And next to the Gayety was

Jimmy Lake's Saloon. Jimmy Lake was the impresario of the Gayety. He occasionally came on stage and introduced one of the burlesque queens. He was proud to report that Justice Holmes, when he came to Washington, found his way to the Gayety.

The Gayety found its way into local law at *4934 Inc. v. Mayor Washington*, 375 A.2d 20. For those of you homesick for Boston, you will enjoy footnote 8:

> *Last, we'll head for Lock-Ober's,*
> > *the Copley or the Ritz*
> *And wish the dear old Howard*
> > *had beat the building blitz.*

If you're not from Boston, you should know that the old Howard was Boston's Gayety.

Jimmy Lake's obituary appeared in the *Washington Post* on September 17, 1967. I saved the obituary. I have it in front of me as I write. Let me quote from it:

> Back in 1960, when Mr. Lake was 80, his back and wrist were broken in a fracas that followed a wrestling match he had announced. For three weeks, according to him, he was unconscious in an oxygen tent in Washington Hospital Center, his fever hovering around 105 degrees.
>
> "I woke up one morning and looked around," he said. "I saw this nurse sitting there. She was beautiful. I gazed at her a bit and my thoughts became corrupt. 'What time is it,' I asked her, and she said it was 3 a.m. 'You had better be going then,' I told her."

In Jimmy's day his saloon and the Gayety Burlesk were the upper hub of Ninth Street. Across the street was the New England

Restaurant. Jimmy usually stayed on his own side of the street. However, on a spring day he would walk across to what was called the New England Beach, the sidewalk in front of the New England. The people on the beach taking the sun were plainclothes detectives, lawyers of some prominence such as Nick Chase, an occasional judge, visiting theatrical people, full-time character witnesses, and well-dressed, respectable bookmakers. When Jimmy Lake went from his side of the street over to the Beach he was received as a visiting celebrity from a faraway land.

There were stores on Ninth Street that had been in existence for many, many years. They were like hardware stores that you occasionally see on the Upper West Side of New York where you can find literally anything. There were pitchmen on the street selling magic tricks and unbelievably sharp glass cutters and a special type of lanolin hair tonic guaranteed to grow hair.

Hodges restaurant was on lower Ninth Street. It was popular with lawyers. Behind the counter was a man in a white suit holding a big saber knife poised above a huge piece of beef. The customer was invited to point to the cut he wanted. The beef was sliced and delicately lifted on the tip of the blade and deposited with a flourish on a soft roll.

I hope next week to drop in on the Spy Museum with my friend Plato, who is an authority on spies. If we have time, we shall stroll down Ninth Street and recall what once was and is no more.

THE COLUMBIAN
BUILDING

Oft in the stilly night,
Ere Slumber's chain hath bound me,
Fond memory brings the light
Of other days around me.

Thomas Moore

No doubt Washington, D.C., will call you at one time or another in your career. It may be an argument before the Supreme Court of the United States. It may be litigation in the United States District Court or the United States Court of Appeals for the District of Columbia. Or it may be profitable business with one of the administrative agencies. No matter. The forthcoming year may well find you wandering around that part of Washington where the courts are located. In your passage from your place of appointment, you could walk past the site of Daniel Webster's old office at Fifth and D streets. From there it is a short walk up Fifth Street. Now look to your left. You see the old gray office building which was once a busy house of activity? The throng of lawyers and clients was there—the quick pulse of loss and gain through lawsuits.

And although some activity continues, the soul has long since fled. Within the building may still be seen the old woodwork and the large offices with the old-style high ceilings, now all but deserted. Within the inner offices are still to be found long, worm-eaten tables, with tarnished gilt leather coverings, supporting ink-stands long since dry. The oaken wainscots are hung with oaken framed pictures of judges who died when the city was young. There they hang, behind thick panes of glass, their chins resting on starched collars decorated below with loosely strung black ties.

Such was the Columbian Building, a magnificent relic when I last examined its interior with care some 30 years ago. The precise alterations that may have been made since, I have had no special opportunity to verify. Time, I take for granted, has not refreshed it.

Situated as it is in the heart of the legal community, it gazes down on Judiciary Square—a grass plot bordered by old and new courthouse buildings. Years ago, the Georgetown University Law School occupied a nearby red-brick building. This great law school cast many callow youths into the stream of people who circulated along Fifth Street. In those days when the Columbian Building flourished, Fifth Street was the rialto of Washington's legal activity.

The lawyers whose offices were within the Columbian Building pushed to the outer limits the custom that sanctioned the publicizing through an exterior window sign the great practitioner within. Gazing up at the building in the 1930's and '40's, one could read the window signs as some great marquee carrying the names of those entitled to star billing. The first floor streetside windows carried the biggest and boldest letters the sign painter could manage.

The occupants of the building were uninhibited in their social and professional pursuits. Each cherished his own idiosyncrasies and wore them proudly. Individuality was neither diluted nor effaced by membership in a large firm. The Columbian Building was a microcosm in which the most exotic styles of advocacy flowered and flourished.

On full display was Robert Ingersoll Miller, who looked like a cross between President Warren G. Harding and a Kentucky colonel and who was always surrounded by a cloud of clients. Bob Miller's fame dated to February 21, 1944, when he shot and killed Dr. John F. Lind, a psychiatrist who was having an affair with Miller's 42-year-old wife. Miller, 67 at the time, confronted them both in front of Woodward & Lothrop department store on F Street, where he shot Dr. Lind.

Miller was indicted for first-degree murder and tried in May 1944. Appearing as a defense witness for her husband, Mrs. Miller testified that he had acted in self-defense. She expressed deep love and affection for him. The jury was out ten minutes before acquitting.

Thereafter, Miller had all the criminal business he could handle. If he could admit to killing a man in broad daylight in front of Woodies and then get himself acquitted, Robert I. Miller was the man to see.

Also in this building was Charles Ford, who did not consider he had given full measure to his client unless the courtroom shook with oratory.

Ford was at his best denouncing government informers and unindicted co-conspirators. He shrieked his denunciations and oftentimes delivered himself of his remarks while standing behind his defendant with hands placed on the defendant's shoulders.

One of Mr. Ford's unforgettable performances was in a hopeless first-degree murder case. In a dramatic gesture he turned on his own client and recounted the evidence against him, albeit in a highly editorialized version. He pointed an accusatory finger at the client and shouted with malice and aforethought, "You manslaughterer! You are guilty of manslaughter and this jury shall convict you of manslaughter!" The jury ignored the evidence of premeditation, the evidence concerning the defendant's making a threat and then going to get the gun and returning and committing the murder. The jury took the cue and brought in a verdict of manslaughter.

Mr. Ford, as most members of the Columbian Building Bar, completed his working day around mid-afternoon. Thus he had a little too much time on his hands and he contracted the gambling habit. He earned large sums of money and he gambled away a good bit of it. During his final illness, one of his friends leaned over the bed and suggested to Mr. Ford that if he had it to do over again, he would not gamble such high stakes. Mr. Ford's response to this homily was, "Have you ever seen a Brinks truck in a funeral procession?"

In contrast to Charles Ford's screaming there was Denny Hughes's whispering. Earlier in his life he was a championship prizefighter, and in the course of his career suffered a broken jaw. Some said that Denny's recovery from his broken jaw was incomplete and he failed to regain the full range of mandibular motion. This had two consequences. Denny gradually converted to a liquid diet and he adopted a most restrained forensic style.

Each working morning Denny left his office and walked across Fifth Street to the police court. Trailing behind him were four or five assorted gamblers who represented the harvest of the previous night's police activity.

Denny was so successful in disposing of these cases by small fine that his clients came to believe Denny was a semi-official licensing agent who would bring in the subject once a year to obtain licensing after a plea of guilty with an explanation.

In one of the few cases Denny actually tried, he brought out on cross-examination that the raiding police had destroyed hundreds of numbers slips. In his closing argument Denny brought to the jury's attention that the widows and orphans who played the numbers were entitled to more consideration than the police gave. The police knew that the destruction of these numbers slips made it impossible for those who hit the number to collect on the bet. As Denny put it, this was a much more serious crime than that for which the defendants were being tried. These destructive police someday must answer for this to the highest authority.

And let us not forget Fred Lane. He was under the influence of the urbane English school of advocacy. He carefully analyzed the evidence in a detached methodical way. This is illustrated by a rape case in which Mr. Lane brought out from the complaining witness through a detailed examination of her that there was little evidence of actual fulfillment. He drove this point home to the jury in his studied way, and then posed the rhetorical question, "Why hasn't the prosecutor shown you the spermatozoa? Where is the spermatozoa?"

Much remains to tell. Many fantastic shapes rise up of those lawyers who live only in memory. Once the memories are stirred, how can I leave out that strange creature T. Edward O'Connell who commenced earning a living as a sign painter on windows of the Columbian Building? Through attendance at night school he obtained his law degree and entered the profession, bringing to it a wardrobe which once seen was not forgotten. Did he purchase those splendid vests, as he claimed, in London's Burlington Arcade?

And what of David Smith, whom fate transported from the Columbian Building to Japan as defense counsel for a Japanese general in the War Crimes trial? I can see Dave now, dressed in black, his reddish hair parted in the middle. He can call from memory all the appellate decisions by volume and number and dismisses *Shepard's Citations* as a superfluous luxury.

And mention must be made of the bondsmen who congregated on the sidewalk in front of the Columbian Building and who carried on a healthy, economically rewarding, symbiotic relationship with the bar.

Then there was the lovely woman who stood across the street in Judiciary Square. Although she was stark-naked and painted all over in gold, nobody gave her much of a look. She had been there so long that she had become part of the scenery. She is there still, while all the rest—Bob Miller, Charlie Ford, Denny Hughes, even the Columbian Building—are gone.

I saw the woman last Sunday as I jogged through the square. She is life-sized, accompanied by a fawn—nymph and fawn, the classical combination. Both stand on a pedestal in the remains of a fountain that was put in place in 1923 and is known as the Joseph J. Darlington Memorial Fountain.

Born in Due West, S.C., in 1849, Darlington came to Washington as a young man, attended law school, and then took an office on Fifth Street, where he established himself as a leader of the legal community. He remained on Fifth Street his whole career. Shortly after his death, friends commissioned a memorial to be erected in his honor, but the design turned out to be somewhat of a surprise. When the nymph's nudity triggered a protest, the sculptor, Carl Paul Jennewein, replied that the lady was "direct from the hand of God instead of from the hands of a dressmaker."

Darlington's greatest successes were in the trial courts, but the U.S. Court of Appeals often reversed cases he had won and sent them back for retrial. Perhaps, one of Darlington's friends noted, that is why the nymph's behind faces the old U.S. Court of Appeals.

Gilt is peeling off the statue now, and the fountain is in need of repair. There are those who deplore the fact that the only memorial in Washington erected to the memory of a working lawyer has lost its luster. The statue must be regilded or buffed down to its bronze, they say. Committees are forming, and the hope is that the nymph of Fifth Street will be restored to her pristine beauty.

But now it is time to close—night's wheels are rattling fast over me. It is proper to have done with this calling forth of the ghosts. In their time they were the carriers of the torch. It was they who performed in accordance with the principles of Cicero and Quintilian. All are now gone and soon even those of us who recall them will be gone. Art is long, life is short.

SUCCESS

Success in the practice of law. What is it? How does one measure it? Place a template identifying your values over what you do and how you do it, and you can give yourself a grade.

Louis Auchincloss in his law-firm novels does just that. The values of his fictional lawyers are the worldly values of practitioners in the influential New York firms during the 1930's. Mr. Auchincloss gives no explicit definition of the worldly values. His characters provide the definition.

Samuel Shellabarger in his biography of Lord Chesterfield (1694–1773) is explicit. He says worldliness is a belief in the supreme desirability of what most people strive for—power, position, wealth, the esteem of one's associates, and the pleasures of the senses. It presents itself in a code of good form and polished civility. Its tactics are an adeptness at compromise, expediency, the unburned bridge, the secret reservation, and a firm belief that ready cash is the best defense against the whips and scorn of time, the oppressor's wrong, and the proud man's contumely. As Shellabarger says: "[T]he objectives of worldliness will always commend themselves to that legal fiction, the ordinary prudent man; its values will always seem valuable to 99 per cent of the population; it is the most plausible form of selfishness."

There are many examples of such success. Take the career of Joseph H. Choate. At the turn of the century he was the trial lawyer of first choice both in New York City, where he resided, and nationally. He tried every type of case, civil, criminal, matrimonial, patent, and personal injury. He contended, before the Supreme Court of the United States, that the income tax law was unconstitutional. He prevailed, and so the Sixteenth Amendment to the Constitution. In 1899 he was appointed United States ambassador to Great Britain. After six years as the ambassador, he resumed his law practice. He was, in the worldly definition, a complete success.

Joseph H. Choate has long since been forgotten. The only trace that is left is a footnote at page 266 of *Prosser's Law of Torts* (5th ed. 1984), citing the case of *Laidlaw v. Sage*, 158 N.Y. 73, 52 N.E. 679 (1899). It represents a case Choate lost. In its time it was a celebrated case.

It commenced on December 4, 1891. On that Friday, Russell Sage, a flint-hearted multimillionaire, was in his bare office near Wall Street in New York City. Sage had made millions through stock market speculation. He refused to use some of his money, as others did, to create an aura of altruism. He was unwilling to spend even a penny to disguise himself and conceal the fact that he was a stingy, greedy man who wanted more money than anybody else. One contemporary interview quoted him as saying: "When you've made your money it is time enough to think of spending it." He was many times a millionaire when he uttered these remarks, but he did not feel the time had come for him to switch from take to give.

Unknown to Sage, a man named Norcross decided *ex parte* that Sage was going to make a substantial departure from his habits of frugality. Norcross wrote out a note that read: "This carpetbag I hold in my hand contains 10 pounds of dynamite, and if I drop this bag on the floor it will destroy this building and kill every human being in it. I demand twelve hundred thousand dollars or I will drop it. Will you give it? Yes or no?"

Norcross implemented his scheme by buying 10 pounds of dynamite and going to Sage's office. When he arrived, Norcross misrepresented that he was on the business of John D. Rockefeller. This ruse quickly brought him into Sage's presence.

Norcross handed Sage the note demanding the money. Sage stood considering the note. Norcross then said: "Then you decline my proposition? Will you give it to me? Yes or no?" Just at this time William R. Laidlaw, Jr., a business visitor, entered the room. He was unaware of the drama in progress.

According to Laidlaw's trial testimony, Sage edged towards him and in a surprisingly warm gesture of hospitality, Sage took Laidlaw's left hand with both his own hands and moved Laidlaw into a position between Sage and Norcross. Sage then said to Norcross: "If you don't trust me, how can you expect me to trust you?"

In a moment there was a terrible explosion. Norcross was blown to bits. Laidlaw was found unconscious, lying on Sage.

Approximately six months later on May 26, 1892, Laidlaw filed suit against Sage. Joseph Choate represented Laidlaw. In the complaint Choate charged that Sage had used Laidlaw as a human shield against the explosion and that, as a proximate result, Laidlaw had suffered serious permanent injuries.

Sage's counsel did not press the defense of contributory negligence. He concentrated on the fact that the explosion was the real cause of any injuries that Laidlaw suffered. The complaint was dismissed because the trial judge held there was no showing of proximate cause between Sage's actions and Laidlaw's injuries. On appeal the trial court was reversed. In reversing, the appellate court held that no question of proximate cause was involved; that if the defendant, Sage, put his hand upon or touched the plaintiff, Laidlaw, and caused him to change his position with an intent to shield himself, he was guilty of a wrongful act towards him; that, if the plaintiff was injured by the happening of the catastrophe, the burden of proof was upon the defendant to establish the fact that his wrongful act did not in the slightest degree contribute any part of the injury the plaintiff sustained by reason of the explosion.

The case was returned for trial. The jury rendered a verdict for the plaintiff in the sum of $25,000. Big money in those days.

Apparently Choate could not resist falling in with the general attack on Sage's stinginess. His cross-examination of Sage, which was challenged by the appellate court, was so entertaining that Francis L. Wellman included specimens of it in *The Art of Cross Examination*. Here is a sample from Wellman:

> Mr. Choate: Were your glasses hurt by the explosion which inflicted forty-seven wounds on your chest?
>
> Mr. Sage: I do not remember.
>
> Mr. Choate: You certainly would remember if you had to buy a new pair.

As part of Sage's trial strategy he wished to imply that he, too, was injured by the explosion. He produced medical testimony

presence of a terrible danger, he is not liable to the plaintiff for the consequences of it." On this second appeal, the appellate court again reversed upon the ground that the court should have charged the jury as requested.

The case was returned for trial again. The third trial found the jury unable to agree, and no verdict was returned. The fourth trial concluded on June 19, 1895, almost four years after the event, with a verdict of $40,000 for Laidlaw.

Sage, unwilling to satisfy the judgment, began another upward movement though the New York appellate superstructure. The intermediary appellate courts for the State of New York sustained the verdict for Laidlaw. Undaunted, Sage pushed his case to the highest Court of Appeals for the State of New York, arriving there in January 1899, some seven years after Norcross's dynamite had exploded. This court became convinced of the wisdom of Sage's defense and held that there was no legally significant relationship between anything Sage did and the injury to Laidlaw. In other words, Laidlaw had failed to carry the burden of proof with respect to proximate cause. Prosser cites *Laidlaw v. Sage* as one of the venerable cases interpreting the rule.

Although the failure to carry the burden of proof was the basis for the reversal, the court took pains to point out that the cross-examination of Sage by Laidlaw's attorney, Joseph H. Choate, went so beyond the bounds that this, too, was a subsidiary ground for reversal.

Oliver Wendell Holmes, in a speech to a bar association, gave his ideas on success in response to a question he posed to himself. "How can the laborious study of a dry and technical system, the greedy watch for clients and practice of shopkeepers arts, the mannerless conflicts over often sordid interests make out a life?" He answered by saying a thinker may live greatly in the law. It is a road to "anthropology, the science of man, to political economy, the theory of legislation, ethics, and thus by several paths to your final view of life."

The biography of Learned Hand demonstrates that he would have been, at best, second-rate if he remained a practicing lawyer. He was not good at getting clients. He liked to take more time to explore the issues than an impatient client thought reasonable. But Judge Hand was a noteworthy success as a trial and appellate judge when measured by Holmes's set of values. His intellectual interests were unbounded. He put them to full use in deciding cases. His biographer describes the pleasure Judge Hand took in exploring the facts of intricate patent and admiralty cases.

There is a set of values tied to the concept of moral courage. A trial practice requires moral courage when it exposes the lawyer to condemnation by those in temporary authority. There are times when establishing a client's rights requires persistence despite a credible threat of contempt or critical comment. Compton Mackenzie, in *Certain Aspects of Moral Courage*, repeats a definition of moral courage set forth by the English barrister James Fitzjames Stephen, who said moral courage is "readiness to expose oneself to suffering an inconvenience which does not affect the body. It arises from firmness of moral principle and is independent of the physical constitution." Compton Mackenzie reports that later, as a judge, Stephen failed to show the required moral courage in a celebrated criminal case over which he presided. He submitted to popular clamor for the conviction of a defendant who probably was innocent.

My example of a lawyer with a good supply of moral courage is Leonard Boudin. His client list included those who were scorned because of their beliefs. Some judges and most congressional investigating committees assumed Mr. Boudin's views were identical to his clients'. Thus he was the target of the same hostility as that directed against the clients. At times the hostility was intense. Mr. Boudin was most comfortable representing the underdog. The person the crowd of the moment despised. So it was when he represented the likes of the Berrigan brothers and Dr. Benjamin Spock. Despite the strong feelings involved in Mr. Boudin's cases, he rarely ended a case without forming a friendship with his opponents.

Now a fourth category of success. In order to get at it, I go to an article entitled "The Pain of Moral Lawyering," by Richard A. Matasar. I came across it on Lexis while looking for something else. Mr. Matasar tells us he left the law practice to teach. He has something to say to us concerning values:

> Every master manipulator of the law also has another voice, an evaluative voice that forms views on the correctness of the client's position. It is the rare lawyer who cannot say with great certainty that he or she has often believed a client's position to be wrong, though arguably acceptable. It is the lawyer's odd lot to argue simultaneously the correctness of matters he or she subjectively believes to be incorrect. Doing so for oneself conjures up images of split personalities and fundamental contradictions. But lawyers suffer no outright schizophrenia, because they argue not for themselves, but as representatives. Though they believe an argument to be incorrect, they make it for their client. Though they may hope the law will not move in a particular direction, for their client's sake they argue, persuasively, to move the law that very way.

Lawyers separate themselves from their clients. It is fundamental to the enterprise. A lawyer who rejects arguments that favor a client's position because the lawyer believes them unsound or wrong is acting as a judge, not as a lawyer. That is not to say that the lawyer does not make judgments about potential arguments for a client, for not every argument that *can* be made *should* be made. Some arguments will not fly, or will put the client in a bad light, or will undermine more important contentions on other parts of the case. This type of judgment is not based on the lawyer's personal beliefs, however. It is cold and impersonal, based on pursuing the client's best interests. The lawyer's own evaluation of the merits of an argument, or more importantly of the wisdom of the client's ends, is held separate, the stuff of idle office chatter, late-night drinks with coworkers, or pillow talk.

Estrangement of lawyers from the positions they must take is an incomplete picture. If it were not, there would be virtually no constraint on the lawyer. After all, the lawyer also could lie on behalf of the client or could omit material facts or contrary authority. But the lawyer cannot do such things because they are unethical. The profession cabins zealous representation with Disciplinary Rules that map the boundary of ethical lawyering.

What a grand success the law practice would be if those of us in the trial practice could spend a few years not with moral pain but with a sense of moral comfort. To do this we must have managed well enough the worldly values to get the money required to buy some freedom. We must have developed a reasonable degree of lawyerly competence by trying cases for the worthy and the unworthy. We must have broadened our vision beyond the day-to-day greedy watch for clients, as Justice Holmes suggests. And we must be ready with moral courage, as needed.

It would be a law practice where we select cases where we are on the right side, the side of the angels. Nevertheless, we would be tolerant of our adversaries' delaying tactics, obfuscation, and needless duplication of papers and pleadings. We know the territory. We know it only too well. That is why we took our leave. When served with the summary judgment motion late Friday, we are amused rather than indignant. In time the merits of the case will overtake the questionable tactics of counsel. We have the mature cynicism described by Lord Chesterfield in a letter to a close friend:

> All the busy tumultuous passions have subsided in me; and that not so much from philosophy, as from a little reflection upon a great deal of experience. I have been behind the scenes, both of pleasure and business. I have seen all the coarse pulleys and dirty ropes, which exhibit and move all the gaudy machines; and I have seen and smelt the tallow candles which illuminate the whole decoration, to the astonishment and admiration of the ignorant audience.

When Lord Chesterfied wrote this, he was looking back on a life filled with accomplishment, some adventure, and a reputation as one of the few honest politicians of his corrupt time. He was not a lawyer. He would have been a good lawyer. He would qualify as one of those whose specialty would be a wisdom practice in addition to his always-on-the-right-side trial practice.

Perhaps we'll call the always-on-the-right-side lawyers the Chesterfield Society. It will consist of the aristocrats of the bar, the select barristers, the chosen. But all attempts to organize them will fail. They will slip through the net. When the door is shut, they are gone. There are no dues and no CLE requirements.

KEEPING SECRETS

Whom a statesman trusts at all he should trust largely, not to say unboundedly; and he should avow his trust to the world. In nine cases out of ten of betrayed confidence in affairs of state, vanity is the traitor. When a man comes into possession of some chance secrets now and then—some one or two—he is tempted to parade them to this friend. But when he is known to be trusted with all manner of secrets, his vanity is interested, not to show them, but to show that he can keep them. And his fidelity of heart is also better secured.

Sir Henry Taylor

Sir Henry makes two points. The first point is obvious. It is the vanity of being known to be trusted with a secret that impels me to disclose it. I prove I am someone of importance by disclosing the secret that someone of established importance has entrusted to me.

Sir Henry's second point is not so obvious. He explains how vanity is used to keep a secret. In order to preserve my reputation as one who can keep a secret, I must not give secrets away. Vanity overcomes vanity.

There is a pleasure in remaining silent when others speak with authority concerning things they don't know about and that I do know about because of secret information. It is the pleasure of certainty held in reserve. It is *prana* pleasure. *Prana* is the vital energy that the yogi masters say rises or falls in accordance with our doing right or doing wrong. The stronger the impulse to tell a secret, the greater the victory in remaining silent and the better the *prana*.

Social beings, as we are, need secrets. We protect ourselves against our enemies with our secrets. Battle plans are highly secret. In World War II the United States broke the Japanese code and Great Britain broke the German code. Winston Churchill said this secret was so valuable that it must be protected by a bodyguard of lies. Secrecy for some is a full-time occupation. Secrecy is in our genes.

Lawyers have a professional obligation to keep secret what their clients tell them. When we become members of the bar, we join an exclusive group that has access to other peoples' secrets. We are in the know.

A lawyer with a good secret is a natural target for a journalist. It is the lawyer's obligation to keep the secret, and it is the journalist's obligation to discover the secret. The journalist relies on flattery to get things moving. The journalist puts in a call to the lawyer. He says he values the lawyer's opinion, the lawyer has a fine reputation, the lawyer is thought to be more competent than other lawyers.

When flattery of this type is administered, the lawyer has no desire to conclude the conversation. Good manners require the lawyer to give something in return for all this flattery. He hints at what he knows. He speaks without attribution, off the record, don't mention me, I will deny it. As the lawyer continues to talk, he hears the clicking of the journalist's computer keyboard.

There is an assumption that skill in keeping secrets comes with the reading of the Rules of Professional Conduct and the cases concerning the attorney-client privilege. Not necessarily so. There are those who are good at keeping client secrets, and there are those who are not so good.

Let me describe a lawyer who was good at keeping secrets. I first met him when he was winding down a long, active career. He had access to the secrets of many people. He had the reputation Sir Henry described, the reputation for keeping secrets. As you might expect, he was a good listener. He did not hint that he knew more than he was permitted to say. He did not assert opinions based on secret knowledge. He told no anecdotes involving his representation of well-known people. His conversation invited what others knew rather than what he knew. For him it was a matter of personal honor to keep secrets, over and above any professional obligation.

The attorney-client privilege commenced long ago in England. It was the barrister's personal honor that was at issue. He would be dishonored if he revealed anything the client told him. Even the client could not order him to reveal what was said. Over time the English judges narrowed the privilege and changed it around to protect the client and not the honor of the lawyer.

In its present form the privilege is sterile. It gives protection only if the client seeks legal advice. People in real trouble need more than strictly legal advice. They need someone to hear them out, in private, with the comfort that what is said will never be revealed. The religious privilege gives this. I hope that some day attorney-client privilege is given the same breadth.

Both privileges require that the parties intend that what is said is to be secret. Both require the secrecy to be absolute. The difference is that the religious privilege provides a protected setting of compassion that an experienced lawyer is well suited to administer. The right lawyer has been known to prevent a suicide attempt, especially if she can suggest that the statute may have run.

Here I quote Wigmore on the religious privilege. "Even assuming that confessions of legal misdeeds continued to be made, the gain would be merely the parties' own confession. This species of evidence ... ought in no system of law be relied on as a chief material object of proof."

The alternative to what I propose would be for lawyers to add a doctorate in divinity to their doctorate in law. A friend of mine, an active local trial lawyer, had both qualifications, theological and legal. She did not worry about the technicalities of the attorney-client privilege. She gave solace as needed. What was not covered by the attorney-client privilege was picked up by the religious privilege. The many who unburdened themselves to her were assured that nothing that was said would be revealed. No time. Not ever. Absolutely never.

One of the reasons lawyers do not keep secrets is the damnable need to advertise for new business. This mitigating circumstance should be weighed against such vulgar indiscretions as client name dropping and hints at secrets that if revealed would change the course of history.

CPSIA information can be obtained at www.ICGtesting.com
Printed in the USA
BVOW08*1137101013

333130BV00001B/1/P